The *flâneur* and his city

Manchester University Press

The *flâneur* and his city
Patterns of daily life in Paris 1815–1851

Richard D. E. Burton

Manchester University Press
Manchester and New York

Copyright © Richard D. E. Burton 1994, 2009

The right of Richard D. E. Burton to be identified as the editor of this work has been asserted by him in accordance with the Copyright, Designs and Patents Act 1988.

Published by Manchester University Press
Oxford Road, Manchester M13 9NR, UK
and Room 400, 175 Fifth Avenue, New York, NY 10010, USA
www.manchesteruniversitypress.co.uk

Distributed exclusively in the USA by
Palgrave, 175 Fifth Avenue, New York NY 10010, USA

Distributed exclusively in Canada by
UBC Press, University of British Columbia, 2029 West Mall,
Vancouver, BC, Canada V6T 1Z2

British Library Cataloguing-in-Publication Data
A catalogue record for this book is available from the British Library

Library of Congress Cataloging-in-Publication Data
A catalog record for this book is available from the Library of Congress

ISBN 13: 978 0 7190 8187 3

First published 1994 by Durham Modern Languages Series
This edition first published 2009 by Manchester University Press

Printed by Lightning Source

CONTENTS

1	The *flâneur*	1
2	Human hieroglyphs: the role of dress in Parisian life	7
3	The rise of the café	15
4	The restaurant	21
5	*Guinguettes, goguettes* and *marchands de vin*	25
6	Shops and shopping	33
7	The omnibus	41
8	*Bals publics*	45
9	Carnival	51
10	*Saltimbanques* and prostitutes	55
11	Conclusion: 'public' and 'private' in pre-1850 Paris	61
	Notes and references	71

Chapter 1
The *Flâneur*

No figure belongs more thoroughly to Paris and to the early nineteenth century than the *flâneur*. That he was as quintessentially 'Parisian' as the *gamin* or the *grisette* was self-evident to contemporaries; 'le flâneur peut naître partout', wrote an anonymous contributor to *Le Livre des cent-et-un* (1831–34), 'il ne sait vivre qu'à Paris'.[1] In *Les Français peints par eux-mêmes* (1840), Auguste de Lacroix was still more forthright: 'Nous n'admettons pas même l'existence du flâneur autre part qu'à Paris'.[2] It was no less self-evident that the *flâneur*, though he may have had late eighteenth century precursors such as Sébastien Mercier and Restif de la Bretonne, was essentially a product of the nineteenth century; the *flâneur*, claimed *Le Livre des cent-et-un*, was not merely the 'premier besoin d'un âge avancé' but 'la plus haute expression de la civilisation moderne'[3] and, as that civilization evolved, so too the *flâneur* underwent a significant mutation, becoming the far more anxious if more 'ecstatic' *homme des foules* of the Second Empire described by Baudelaire. In his pre-1850 form, the *flâneur* was much more than a mere peripatetic observer of Parisian life, and most writers on the subject were at pains to distinguish him from the simple *badaud*. The distinction is not always clear and will become still less so in the second half of the century, but the fundamental opposition is well defined by de Lacroix:

> Le badaud ne pense pas; il ne perçoit les objets qu'extérieurement. Il n'y a pas de communication entre son cerveau et ses sens. Pour lui les choses n'existent que simplement et superficiellement; le coeur humain est un monolithe dont les hiéroglyphes ne l'intéressent nullement.[4]

Despite the superficial analogies between *badauderie* and *flânerie*, the former is essentially passive and affective while the latter is active and intellectual; the *flâneur*, says de Lacroix, is 'l'observateur en action, l'observateur dans son expression la plus élevée et la plus éminemment utile'.[5] The *badaud* absorbs and is absorbed by the flux of urban life and, to that extent, is closer to the Baudelairean *homme des foules* of the Second Empire. The *flâneur*, in contrast, stands apart from the city even as he appears to 'fuse' with it; he interprets each of its component parts in isolation in order, subsequently, to attain to an intellectual understanding of the whole as a complex system of meaning. The distinction is clearly made by Victor Fournel in his *Ce qu'on voit dans les rues de Paris*

(1858), written at a time when the *flâneur* was already beginning to give way before the related but rival figure of the *homme des foules*. According to Fournel, the *flâneur*

> est toujours en pleine possession de son individualité. Celle du badaud disparaît, au contraire, absorbée par le monde extérieur qui le ravit à lui-même, qui le frappe jusqu'à l'enivrement et l'extase. Le badaud, sous l'influence du spectacle, devient un être impersonnel; ce n'est plus un homme: il est public, il est foule.[6]

For the *badaud*, Fournel writes elsewhere, the ebb and flow of urban life is an opiate that delivers him from himself; he experiences 'le *kief* du boulevard' as a quasi-mystic fusion between self and non-self.[7] the rapture of the *flâneur* — which, in its way, is no less intense — is a rapture of understanding which, pushed to its limit, becomes, as we shall see in the case of Balzac, a kind of preternatural illumination based on the interpenetration of knower and known, a privileged state of being in which, however, the cognitive element remains paramount.

In his pre–1850 form, the *flâneur* is first and foremost a 'reader' of urban life. 'Tout est pour lui un texte d'observations', wrote *le Livre des cent-et-un*,[8] but, as de Lacroix implied in his contrast between *badaud* and *flâneur*, that text was 'hieroglyphic' in character, complex, arcane and polysemic, and required a specialized and abnormally acute reader — a Champollion of the city — to decipher its multiple meanings. The *flâneur* is that reader; he alone can interpret and understand the cryptic utterances of 'ce sphinx qu'on appelle Paris' (Alfred Delvau, *Les Dessous de Paris* (1862)),[9] and to this task he devotes, quite simply, every instant of his waking life. For the *flâneur*, Parisian life is before all else a *system of signs* in which even the most trivial phenomenon is replete with meaning, and, if 'read' correctly and linked to other perhaps widely disparate phenomena, will disclose a universe of significance: 'Tout pour moi devient allégorie'. The *flâneur*'s heuristic assumptions are tellingly summarized by a little-known contributor to *Le Livre des cent-et-un*, Charles Lenormant: 'Tout est l'expression de tout'.[10] To describe the *flâneur* as a semiologist *avant la lettre* is in no sense, therefore, to read back into the past preoccupations of the present. On the contrary, the belief that urban life consisted of a multiplicity of interlocking semiotic systems and that everything in the city was, by definition, meaningful was so widespread amongst writers on pre–1850 Paris as to be virtually platitudinous; without such a theory, the countless 'physionomies' and 'physiologies' of urban types that appeared during the period could simply not have been written. Thus in *Les Français peints par eux-mêmes* Taxile Delord stated programmatically that, in Paris, 'tout s'enchaîne et se lie, le sentiment moral d'un siècle se reflète partout, chaque chose qui émane de la masse a sa signification'.[11] Similarly, Delphine de Girardin wrote in 1839 that 'pour nous tout est symptôme. Chaque objet nous révèle une pensée; les détails les plus insignifiants ont un langage que nous entendons'.[12] Once this presumption of meaning has been made, each and every aspect of Parisian life may be subjected to a minute reading that interprets all cultural phenomena as, in some way or other, forms of communication. Thus, describing the typical dancer at the Bal Chicard, Taxile Delord states that

> tous ses mouvements ont un sens, toutes ses contorsions sont des emblèmes; ce que les bras ont indiqué, les yeux achèvent de le dire; les hanches et les reins ont aussi leurs figures de rhétorique, leur éloquence.[13]

Architecture, too, is commonly viewed as a system of meaning. This is true not only of public buildings such as the Bourse or the Panthéon but also, wrote Edmond Texier in his monumental *Tableau de Paris* (1853), of the simplest 'maison bourgeoise' which, although no more than a 'gigantesque commode cubique' to the casual observer, becomes a richly meaningful text when scrutinized by the specialist:

> Pourtant toutes, pour qui sait la lire, portent sur le frontispice leur histoire; mais il n'est pas toujours aisé de déchiffrer les caractères que le temps a gravés. On dirait que les moeurs des habitants laissent sur ces murs une empreinte reconnaissable; ou, pour le moins, des traces qui, combinées avec quelques autres, suffisent pour mettre le moraliste sur la voie, et pour qu'il soit à même de juger le contenu à l'inspection du contenant.[14]

Even a man's gait is seen as a form of communication. In his *Théorie de la démarche* (1833) — a work in which, characteristically, he proposed to 'codifier, faire de code de la démarche' — Balzac advanced the germs of a 'semiological' theory of walking:

> La démarche est la physionomie du corps. N'est-il pas effrayant de penser qu'un observateur profond peut découvrir un vice, un remords, une maladie en voyant un homme en mouvement? Quel riche langage dans ces effets immédiats d'une volonté traduite avec innocence! L'inclination plus ou moins vive d'un de nos membres; la forme télégraphique dont il a contracté, malgré nous, l'habitude; l'angle ou le contour que nous lui faisons décrire, sont empreints de notre vouloir, et sont d'une effrayante signification. C'est plus que la parole, c'est la pensée en action.[15]

Finally, and most memorably, Balzac described clothes in his *Traité de la vie élégante* (1830) as 'l'homme avec le texte de son existence, l'homme hiéroglyphié'[16] and went on to propose a whole new science to be known as *vestignomie* which would enable the observer — instantaneously, for there would be no time to know the 'whole man' — to deduce a whole series of social, political and psychological meanings from the vestimentary signals emitted by those around him. It is hardly surprising, therefore, that Balzac should describe the insights of the *flâneur* or *physionomiste* as 'frightening' (no less, perhaps for their possessor than for their object), since what they involve is nothing less than an almost god-like power-through-knowledge over the Other.

All *physionomies* assume the existence of hieroglyphic 'correspondences' between outward forms and inner realities, correspondences that only the initiate can decipher and which in many, perhaps most, cases remain unknown to the individual or group emitting the cultural message in question. As Walter Benjamin and others have suggested, [17] the *physionomie* (which is essentially the activity of *flânerie* given textual form) is characteristic of an epoch in which, to some extent at least, received social meanings have been disrupted by unprecedented change, in which individuals are becoming progressively more estranged both from each other and from their environment and in which, in consequence, they are in need of specialized but easily assimilated information and techniques to guide them through the increasingly enigmatic and 'illegible' city in which they find themselves. In all this a fundamental importance attaches to the activity of *seeing*, for as George Simmel and, after him, Walter Benjamin and Louis Wirth have insisted, 'interpersonal relationships in big cities are distinguished by a marked preponderance of the activity of the eye over the activity of the ear'.[18] From the *physionomie* the city-dweller — especially, no doubt, the recent arrivant from the provinces — sought not merely skills that would enable him instantly to deduce from outward forms meanings that were no longer inscribed in nature or unchanging custom but also, no doubt, ways in which he himself might avoid emitting those 'tell-tale signs' that would give to others the power that he sought to exercise over them. The *physionomie* implies a shifting social world in which individuals are increasingly objects to each other, in which verbal communication is being supplanted by an anxious 'sizing up' of those around one and in which human relations are, in general, characterized by a prickly unease and latent animosity. The *flâneur* belongs to the same social and moral universe as the spy, the *agent de sûreté* and, somewhat later, the detective. Like them, he strives to be both all-seeing and invisible (though, just as spies were commonly spied upon, so too the *flâneur* is himself not infrequently the object of a *physionomie*) and, no less than Vidocq or Hugo's Javert, he is a Protean figure capable of assuming a variety of disguises in order to pursue his scopophiliac passion undetected. The *flâneur*, Janin wrote in *Un Hiver à Paris* (1843), 'est partout et il n'est nulle part',[19] omnipresent but invisible like the God of the Old testament. In a world in which to see is to know is to wield power, the *flâneur* is the seer *par excellence*. *Voyeur* and *voyant* combined, he begins as a roving empiricist and ends as little less than a visionary.

When pushed to their limit, the visionary powers of the *flâneur* call in question the principle of identity itself. By dint of concentrating on the Other, the observer may, by a transposition or interpenetration of selves, almost become that Other, as in the following truly extraordinary passage in Balzac's *Ficino Cane* (1836):

> Chez moi l'observation était déja devenue intuitive, elle pénétrait l'âme sans négliger le corps; ou plutôt elle saisissait si bien les détails extérieurs, qu'elle allait sur-le-champ au delà; elle me donnait la faculté de vivre de la vie de l'individu sur laquelle elle s'exerçait, en me permettant de me substituer à lui comme le derviche des *Mille et une nuits* prenait le corps et l'âme des personnes sur lesquelles il prononçait certaines paroles. Lorsque, entre onze heures et minuit, je rencontrais un ouvrier et sa femme revenant ensemble de l'Ambigu-Comique, je m'amusais à les suivre depuis le boulevard du Pont-aux-Choux jusqu'au boulevard Beaumarchais. [...] En entendant ces gens, je pouvais épouser leur vie, je me sentais leurs guenilles sur le dos, je marchais les pieds dans leurs souliers percés; leurs désirs, leurs besoins, tout passait dans mon âme, ou mon âme passait dans la leur. C'était le rêve d'un homme éveillé. [...] Quitter ses habitudes, devenir un autre que soi par l'ivresse des facultés morales, et jouer ce jeu à volonté, telle était ma distraction. A quoi dois-je ce don? est-ce une seconde vue? est-ce une des qualités dont l'abus mènerait à la folie? je n'ai jamais recherché les causes de cette puissance; je la possède et m'en sers, voilà tout.[20]

Once this point has been reached, the *flâneur* is already well on the way to becoming the *homme des foules* of the Second Empire and beyond. Whereas the pre–1850 *flâneur* strives to understand the individual Other in his or her otherness, the *homme des foules*, as described by Baudelaire, seeks to lose all selfhood in a quasi-mystic (or quasi-orgasmic) fusion with 'la foule' considered as an undifferentiated and anonymous mass: 'C'est un *moi* insatiable du *non-moi*'.[21] His stance, as we have seen already, is essentially passive while that of the *flâneur*, appearances notwithstanding, is active; the *flâneur* participates in urban life even as he observes it whereas the *homme des foules* is a pure spectator-figure who longs, however, to merge ecstatically with the spectacle before him, a longing that is doomed to eternal frustration for he remains as isolated and imprisoned in self at the end of his odyssey through the Paris streets as he was at the outset. The purposefulness and vigour of the *flâneur* reflect the dynamism and variety of the urban society he observed; the passivity and despair of the *homme des foules* belong, in contrast, to a city in which, as a result of compex social changes, there were, in the memorable phrase of Auguste Cochin that I have cited and discussed elsewhere,[22] no longer any true 'citoyens' but only a mass of scarcely differentiated 'habitants'.

The object of the present essay is to provide a '*flâneur's* eye view' of certain salient features of Parisian life in the first half of the nineteenth century, notably dress, cafés, restaurants and other eating- and drinking-places, shops and *passages*, the omnibus, *bals publics* and carnival, and, from a discussion of these, to arrive at some general conclusions regarding the relationship of 'private' and 'public' spheres of existence in 'le vieux Paris'. Like the *flâneur*, I shall concentrate less on factual information for its own sake — which may be found in the secondary works cited in the text and footnotes — than on the 'semiological' or 'anthropological' significance of the cultural forms in question. In every instance and at every opportunity, I shall endeavour to link cultural institutions to the general pattern of class relations in pre–1850 Paris, stressing both the persistence of cross-class contacts and the growing differentiation between classes. Above all, it will be shown how progress towards legal and political equality was accompanied by growing cultural inequality, how the *rapprochement* of different social groups in the eyes of the law occasioned, as de Tocqueville was the first to perceive, an increasingly sharp separation in terms of concrete behaviour and attitudes. 'Partout, et en toute chose, éclate à Paris les inégalités des conditions, dans ce pays ivre d'égalité', wrote Balzac in *le Cousin Pons* (1847),[23] words that are complemented by the shrewd observation made in 1839 by Delphine de Girardin that the 'besoin d'égalité' and the 'besoin de luxe' that appeared to her to dominate life in the capital were 'deux passions rivales, rivales en apparence, mais associées en réalité, opposées de langage, mais fraternelles d'origine'.[24] The pages that follow aim to demonstrate the pertinence of both these propositions.

Chapter 2
Human hieroglyphs: the role of dress in Parisian life

Dress, as we have seen, was viewed by Balzac as a kind of runic inscription whose meaning only the most practised 'vestignomist' might decipher. To many observers of Parisian life, however, dress presented little problem. Changes had certainly occurred since the *ancien régime*, almost all of them involving greater homogenization and monochromaticism, but these, it seemed, could readily be interpreted in the light of the comparative democratization of French society since 1789. In male dress, the most obvious innovation was the way in which, at the 'upper end' of society, distinction between aristocratic and bourgeois modes of dress had apparently been blurred by the adoption of the *habit noir* by both classes as a kind of social uniform designed to differentiate them *en bloc* from the *blouse*-clad classes beneath them. Commentators had no difficulty in linking this development to wider social, political and economic changes. In *Les Français peints par eux-mêmes* (1840), for example, Roger de Beauvoir stated that 'l'habit noir est devenu la charte universelle; il fera le tour du globe. ... Autrefois la confusion des rangs n'avait pas amené celle du costume, les princes étaient vêtus comme devaient l'être les princes, les bourgeois portaient l'habit de la bourgeoisie'.[1] In the 1830s even Louis Philippe and his courtiers customarily wore the *habit noir* and deputies also relinquished their uniforms in its favour; in the parliamentary debate on the subject in 1838 Thiers voiced the opinion that 'l'habit que tout le monde porte tous les jours est celui qui nous convient le mieux'.[2] A degree of levelling had also taken place between the middle- and lower-class, though the *blouse* was long to remain the distinguishing mark of the working-man. In 1834 the *Journal des femmes* stated that, as a result of mechanization (principally the introduction of the sewing machine in the late 1820s),

> des objets qui jadis n'étaient que le partage des classes riches et aisées deviennent d'un emploi général. Les vêtements sont plus chauds et plus sains. L'ouvrier, autrefois vêtu d'une étoffe grossière, ne porte plus que de l'Elbeuf et du Sedan; ses chemises sont d'un tissu fin et blanc, et ses chaussures légères attestent le progrès de la tannerie.[3]

With the introduction of ready-made clothes (*confectionnement*) in the 1840s, equalization proceeded still further and it was possible for *Le Figaro* to state in 1855 that 'entre l'habit noir de M. Rothschild et l'habit noir de son dernier commis, il n'y a que des nuances imperceptibles qui ne peuvent être appréciées que par un garçon tailleur'.[4] Equalization was to be observed, too, though to a lesser extent and then principally at the 'lower end' of society, in female dress. Writing in 1816, the 'Hermite de la Chaussée-d'Antin' (V.J.E. de Jouy) claimed that

> la fille d'un marchand, d'un promeneur, n'a rien qui la distingue aujourd'hui de celle d'un bon artisan. Leur parure est semblable, leur coiffure est la même ... et ce n'est guère qu'en faisant attention aux hommes qui les accompagnent qu'on peut deviner à quelles classes de la société elles appartiennent.[5]

Although, as *La Mode* stated in 1830, 'la toilette n'est pas étrangère à la politique'[6] and although it was common to sport 'la coiffure dite Juste-Milieu', 'l'œillet rouge républicain' or the 'bousingot' as an index of Orleanist or Republican sentiments, in other respects nineteenth century dress was markedly more impoverished as a semiotic system than had been the case under the *ancien régime*. Many of the distinctive costumes which, in the eighteenth century, had indicated not merely a person's class but his or her actual profession had disappeared and, although children's dress was now entirely *sui generis* and no longer a miniature version of adult costume, earlier vestimentary distinctions between different age-groups had also succumbed to the general process of homogenization. In 1831 Charles Lenormant wrote that

> les vieillards en sont venus peu à peu à ressembler beaucoup trop aux jeunes gens. De même qu'en 1730, il n'y avait que de petits hommes, et point d'enfants, de même aujourd'hui il n'y a que de vieux jeunes gens et point de vieillards.[7]

The complex class, professional and generational distinctions that had obtained in eighteenth century dress seemed, at least as far as men were concerned, to have been supplanted by a single gross distinction between middle- and upper-class *habit* on the one hand and lower-class *blouse* on the other. There could be no doubt, wrote Lenormant, of 'la tendance démocratique de notre costume actuel'.[8]

To the *flâneur*, however, such a reading of the language of clothes took account of only the most obvious changes. Beneath the surface homogeneity a myriad of subtle distinctions could be discerned. To start with, wrote Montigny in *Le Provincial à Paris* (1826), it *was* still possible to distinguish between different professions and even between members of the same profession operating in different *quartiers*, not, to be sure, on the basis of the immediately comprehensible 'uniforms' of the *ancien régime*, but by noting certain vestimentary peculiarities that would forever escape the non-initiate:

> On prétend que tout le monde étant vêtu de même, il est maintenant impossible de deviner la profession à l'inspection de leur costume: regardez, regardez bien, et vous apercevrez distinctement certaines nuances, certaines habitudes du corps qui d'abord peuvent échapper. L'artisan, le propriétaire, le négociant, l'employé, ont des manières qui leur sont propres. A l'heure de dîner ou à celle de se reposer, toutes ces gens se classent selon leurs goûts, leurs habitudes, leurs prétentions. ... Tel métier, telle corporation a son luxe et ses manières de se parer et de se vêtir. Entrez, dans la même journée, chez un bijoutier de la rue Vivienne et chez un orfèvre de la halle: examinez l'étalage d'un marchand de nouveautés du Boulevard Italien, et celui d'un de ses confrères du faubourg Saint-Antoine, et vous apercevrez une différence égale à celle qui distingue un Provincial en retard d'un Parisien qui s'attelle en esclave au char brillant de la mode.[9]

After the Revolution of 1830 and the final blurring (or so it seemed) of the distinction between aristocracy and upper bourgeoisie, such indices of status and profession became still more difficult to detect, whence the demand for 'vestignomies' which would enable the individual to 'read' the increasingly neutral and monosemic dress of the Bourgeois Monarchy. Not surprisingly, it is the first of such works, Balzac's *Traité de la vie élégante*, that gives the most subtle analysis of the relationship between class, individuality and dress and of the way in which the accomplished observer may distinguish between persons and groups despite the apparent uniformity of their dress. Balzac's theory may be rephrased and summarized as follows. The social distinctions of the eighteenth century — and particularly those between the aristocratic leisure-class and the bourgeoisie — were obvious and immediately visible, and the vestimentary language in which they were expressed was likewise instantaneously legible; in semiological terms, the relationship between signifier and signified was direct, unproblematic and 'natural'. As a result, however, of the undoubted *formal* and *legal* equalities that had emerged since 1789, the relationship between dress, class and individuality had become exceptionally complex, not because of an increase in the number of vestimentary signifiers but precisely because of their reduction; the principle of interchangeability that I have commented on elsewhere in the realm of architecture[10] appeared to dominate dress as well, and the link between signifier and signified now seemed wholly arbitrary. The old tripartite distinction between aristocracy, bourgeoisie and lower classes had apparently been superseded by a crude opposition between two undifferentiated groups, 'les riches et les pauvres, les gens en voiture et les gens à pied, ceux qui ont payé le droit d'être oisifs et ceux qui tentent de l'acquérir'.[11] In the face of this homogenisation, 'elegance', says Balzac, is no longer a matter of class affiliation but of individual temperament and genius, less a sign, as it was under the *ancien régime*, of the economic and social power of a hereditary leisure-class than of the personal superiority of the exceptional individual. The *embourgeoisement* of society and its dress creates the dandy who, whatever his class by birth, aspires, through his mastery of the language of dress, to a kind of spiritual aristocracy which, according to Balzac, is taking the place of the old, decaying social aristocracy:

> Du moment que ... le fils naturel d'un baigneur millionnaire et un homme de talent ont les mêmes droits que le fils d'un comte, nous ne pouvons plus être distinctibles que par notre valeur intrinsèque. Alors, dans notre société, les différences ont disparu: il n'y a plus que des nuances. Aussi le savoir-vivre, l'élégance des manières, le *je ne sais quoi*, fruit d'une éducation complète, forment la seule barrière qui sépare l'oisif de l'homme occupé. S'il existe un privilège, il dérive de la supériorité morale. De là le haut prix attaché ... à l'instruction, à la pureté du langage, à la grâce du maintien, à la manière plus ou moins aisée dont une toilette est portée, à la recherche des appartements, enfin à la perfection de tout ce qui procède de la personne. N'imprimons-nous pas nos mœurs, notre pensée, sur tout ce qui nous entoure et nous appartient? Parle, marche, mange ou habille-toi, et je te dirai qui tu es a remplacé l'ancien proverbe, expression de cour, adage de privilégié.[12]

Much the same argument was to be advanced later by Baudelaire in *Le Peintre de la vie moderne* (1863) where dandyism — a product, says Baudelaire, of those 'époques transitoires où la démocratie n'est pas encore toute-puissante, où l'aristocratie n'est que partiellement chancelante et avilie' — is seen as an attempt by 'quelques hommes déclassés, dégoûtés, désœuvrés, mais tous riches de force native' to establish 'une espèce nouvelle d'aristocratie, d'autant plus difficile à rompre qu'elle sera basée sur les facultés les plus précieuses, les plus indestructibles, et sur les dons célestes que le travail et l'argent ne peuvent conférer'.[13] Dandyism, Roger Kempf has written, is 'un culte de la différence dans le siècle de l'uniforme'.[14] Nonetheless, the dandy does not seek to flout the vestimentary norms of bourgeois society by a conspicuous lavishness that would be obvious to all and sundry. Rather is he motivated, says Baudelaire, by 'le besoin ardent de se faire une originalité, contenu dans les limites extérieures des convenances',[15] aiming, in Balzac's words, to 'ne rien faire comme les autres, en paraissant faire tout comme eux'.[16] Like every other male of aristocratic or upper middle-class (even middle-class) status, he wears the *habit noir*, the *redingote* and the *chapeau haut-de-forme*; his *cravate* is not loud nor does he indulge in provocative solecisms such as the scarlet waistcoat worn by Gautier at the first night of *Hernani*. Only the fellow 'cultist' can recognize him for what he is. It is no longer the obvious expense of clothes that constitutes 'élégance' as it was under the *ancien régime*, but style, cut and the quintessence of personality simultaneously concealed and revealed by the subtle harmony of the ensemble. Dandyism, Baudelaire avers, is 'une espèce de culte de soi-même';[17] it is introverted (though dependent on recognition by a kindred Other), ascetic and asexual (even antisexual), the very antithesis of the extroverted and highly erotic lavishness of old-style elegance. Nonetheless, dandyism defies bourgeois norms even as it appears to endorse them. It is above all the *time* devoted to the creation of the ensemble that distinguishes the dandy from the 'time is money' ethos of the bourgeois majority. Adapting and expanding Roger Kempf's definition, we may say that dandyism is the cult of the useless in an age of utilitarianism.

But the dandy was, by definition, an exception, and it may be that he has received more attention, both from contemporaries and later commentators, than his social importance warrants. It is more pertinent to our general purpose to investigate the social 'message' that, consciously or unconsciously, the ordinary middle-class man and woman expressed through their dress in pre-1850 Paris. Following Quentin Bell[18] (who in his turn bases his argument on Veblen's *Theory of the Leisure Class*) we may say that the over-riding preoccupation of the middle-class man was to differentiate himself from those who obtained their livelihood through *manual* labour. In 1829 *La Mode* criticized the wearing of 'la demi-botte serrée dans les pantalons larges' on the grounds that 'cela ne convient qu'aux ouvriers et à ceux qui sont continuellement exposés à la boue des rues et qui ne peuvent changer beaucoup de vêtements; l'autre chaussure distingue d'une manière convenable les personnes d'un rang plus élevé'. Distinction, continued *La Mode*, is 'toujours assurée par l'adoption d'un vêtement large' whereas the *habillement serré* 'vient des classes inférieures et principalement des artisans et du bas commerce. Pourquoi? C'est que l'ancien habillement serré est proprement celui qui leur convient; car tout disgracieux et tout ridicule qu'il est, comme il s'adapte à la peau, il les expose moins aux taches durant leur travail'. The conclusion was obvious: 'Que l'artisan et l'ouvrier se contentent d'un vêtement étroit et fait pour le travail et que les autres s'attachent à un costume plus relevé'.[19] On the other hand, the middle-class man was equally anxious, particularly during the Restoration period, to indicate that, unlike the leisured aristocracy, he was an active, productive and useful member of society, intent upon economy rather than conspicuous consumption. As such, he eschewed the needlessly expensive, artificial and work-inhibiting opulence sought by the old aristocracy, seeking instead a modest and restrained appearance that would express his fundamental seriousness of purpose: 'Tout concourt à rendre notre costume plus sérieux et plus naturel,' wrote Lenormant in *Le Livre des cent-et-un*.[20] The *habit noir* fulfilled all these *desiderata*. Its sobriety indicated unambiguously that its wearer was not the frivolous member of a parasitical leisure-class and, while it permitted non-manual work, the importance attached to impeccable starched cuffs and collars, immaculately pressed trousers and spotless shoes guaranteed that no manual work could be undertaken; the one 'ornament' permitted — the gold watch-chain — was itself highly functional and clearly demonstrated the importance of time in the bourgeois *Weltanschauung*. There could be no greater contrast to the lavish, extroverted dress of the old aristocracy than the sombre — indeed funereal garb — described by Baudelaire in his *Salon* of 1846:

> N'est-il pas l'habit nécessaire de notre époque, souffrante et portant jusque sur ses épaules noires et maigres le symbole d'un deuil perpétuel? Remarquez bien que l'habit noir et la redingote ont non seulement leur beauté politique, qui est l'expression de l'égalité universelle, mais encore leur beauté poétique, qui est l'expression de l'âme publique;- une immense défilade de croque-morts, croque-morts politiques, croque-morts amoureux, croque-morts bourgeois. Nous célébrons tous quelque enterrement.[21]

Not for nothing do Daumier's countless bourgeois males appear as everywhere and at all times identical to each other, as though cloned *ad infinitum* from a single slightly corpulent, dark-suited genotype. At a time when the bourgeoisie was beginning consciously to segregate itself from other classes, the *habit noir* functioned almost as a bastion into which the middle-class man could retreat away from the probing eye of the Other. On the one hand, it designated him unambiguously as bourgeois (which had obvious disadvantages on occasions of popular turbulence) while, on the other, its deliberately neutral appearance, its interchangeability with all other *habits noirs*, rendered him comparatively illegible, even invisible, as an individual. In revealing him as the member of a class, it concealed him individually.

The situation of the middle-class woman was rather more complex, and, unlike that of her male counterpart whose dress remained remarkably constant throughout the first half of the century (and indeed throughout the whole century), was to undergo a significant evolution during the period in question. During the Restoration and early years of the Bourgeois Monarchy, the very wealthiest *bourgeoises* (those, notably, of the Chaussée-d'Antin) sought, as a reading of *Le Père Goriot* makes abundantly clear, to emulate the aristocratic fashions of the Faubourg Saint-Germain. But this emulation involved only an extremely small minority and until the mid 1830s the dress of most upper middle-class (and certainly all middle-class) women, no less than that of middle-class men, emphasized economy, restraint and seriousness. This style of dress coincided with and expressed a particular stage of the history of the Parisian bourgeoisie when it was engaged in defining itself over and against what it saw as, on the one hand, a spendthrift aristocracy and, on the other, an improvident populace and when, in general, the need to accumulate capital dictated the avoidance of ostentatious expense. By the mid to late 1830s, however, the wealthier sections of the Parisian bourgeoisie (and not merely the élite of the Chaussée-d'Antin), their position now secure, began, like the aristocracy they had largely supplanted, to wish to display their economic and social power. Middle-class males could not adopt a more extravagant mode of dress without undermining their collective self-image as industrious and serious-minded members of society, and accordingly it was wives and daughters who were charged with the task of demonstrating the family's wealth and power through their dress. Just as middle-class interiors became markedly more lavish from the mid-1830s onwards,[22] so female fashion became more opulent and extroverted at precisely the same time. The transformation, was swiftly noted by the ever-alert Delphine de Girardin when she recorded in December 1838 that 'la mode des riches étoffes est revenue'. For some years previously, she continued, 'les grandes parures ressemblaient à des demi- négligés, les robes de bal étaient franchement des robes de dessous; les chapeaux habillés étaient de naïves capotes de pensionnaires'. The upper middle-class was beginning to imitate the styles of the aristocracy against which it had previously been so anxious to contra-distinguish itself: 'Les modes sont royales, et comme les mœurs sont toujours très bourgeoises, les dépenses n'ont plus be bornes'.[23] In April 1839 she gave the following analysis of the transformation:

> Les modes doivent inévitablement varier selon l'âge et la position, et s'amender selon les fortunes, selon les quartiers, selon les habitudes, selon les figures et les tournures, selon les circonstances et même selon les événements de la vie. La mode en ce moment est de garnir les robes de six, sept et huit volants ... Qu'une merveilleuse de la Chaussée d'Antin aille au bal chez un banquier de l'ex-rue du Mont-Blanc, parée d'une robe garnie de la sorte, on la trouvera charmante; les huits volants seront là, non seulement appréciés, mais enviés par toutes les robes rivales qui n'auront que quatre, cinq et six volants. En avoir huit, c'est dire: je fais les choses plus grandement que vous; je suis élégante au huitième degré; j'ai de plus que vous deux quartiers de noblesse; je m'estime et je vaux deux volants de plus que vous.[24]

By 1840 the fashion for the extravagant and the superfluous had developed still further:

> Aujourd'hui, la fureur des ornements est poussée jusqu'à la démence. Ce sont des volants sans nombre et hors de toutes proportions; ce sont des flots de dentelle, des nuages de marabouts, des bosquets de fleurs, des inondations de diamants.[25]

The contrast between the female fashions of the 1820s and those of the late 1830s and early 1840s mirrors exactly the contrast made by Balzac in *La Cousine Bette* between 'l'Opposition bourgeoise' (represented by César Birotteau) and 'la triomphante bourgeoisie' (represented by Birotteau's successor, Crevel): 'Dans les révolutions comme dans les tempêtes maritimes, les valeurs solides vont à fond, le flot met les choses légères à fleur d'eau'.[26] In contrast to the economical, 'inner-directed' bourgeoisie of the earlier period, the upper middle-classes of the 1840s were increasingly 'other-directed' and expansive in their life-styles and as far as female fashions were concerned, the situation was already well advanced towards that of the Second Empire when, as *L'Illustration* stated in 1862, 'la femme est devenue une façon de vaniteux étalage ... Le cachemire crie: je coûte dix mille francs ... La femme est une plus-value que l'on pourrait côter à la Bourse'.[26]

Chapter 3
The Rise of the Café

The café was by no means a nineteenth century invention — the Café Procope had been founded in 1686 and, according to François Fosca's *Histoire des cafés de Paris*, there were 380 cafés in the capital in 1723 and as many as 1800 on the eve of the Revolution[1] — but it was only during the nineteenth century that the café became a fundamental institution of Parisian culture. By 1807 the number of cafés had increased to around 4000 and by the 1850s was, on Victor Fournel's evidence, a ubiquitous feature of the Paris streets:

> Le café s'est fourré partout; il vous poursuit dans les ruelles et les impasses, les galeries et les passages, au bal, au théâtre, à l'exposition, aux bains, aux concerts, sur les quais, sur les ponts même. On ne peut fuir le café.[2]

The phenomenal increase in the number of cafés was caused by and expressed a series of complex social, political and economic changes which are well summarized in an incisive passage in Antoine Caillot's *Mémoires pour servir à l'histoire des moeurs et usages des Français* (1827). Before the Revolution, claimed Caillot, the growth of cafés was inhibited by 'le peu d'intérêt qu'on prenait aux affaires publiques', by 'la rareté des relations commerciales' and by 'l'habitude où étaient un grand nombre de bourgeois de prendre chez eux le café'. All this was changed by the upheaval of French, and particularly Parisian, society in 1789:

> Mais, lorsque la révolution eut fait naître des intérêts politiques pour toutes les professions, et appelé les citoyens à délibérer sur ces mêmes intérêts; lorsque la création de la garde nationale les eut réunis sous les mêmes drapeaux; que la liberté de la presse eut augmenté le nombre des feuilles publiques …, que ce fut devenu pour tous un besoin de se mettre au courant des événements, et que l'esprit militaire eut accoutumé les bourgeois à quitter le *corps-de-garde* pour aller *boire la goutte*, ou prendre la demi-tasse, les cafés déjà établis ne suffisant plus aux nouveaux besoins, il fallut bien qu'il s'en établît un plus grand nombre. Aussi dans presque toutes les rues, sur les quais et les places publiques de la capitale il s'en ouvrit successivement qui bientôt, le matin et le soir, se remplirent de citoyens de tous les états, et devinrent comme autant de cabinets de lecture, par le grand nombre de journaux qu'il leur fallut offrir à la curiosité publique. Tous ces cafés s'embellirent, plus ou moins, de glaces et d'autres ornements à la mode.[3]

The café, wrote the Goncourt brothers in their study of the Directoire, was the concrete expression and focus of the 'sociability' — the immensely heightened concern for public affairs and the desire for dynamic interchange with others — unleashed by the Revolution:

> A peine née, la révolution pousse les hommes les uns contre les autres, les assemble, frotte les idées contre les idées, les paroles contre les paroles, pour, de ces associations et de ces chocs, faire jaillir la flamme, l'éclair, la liberté. Un grand besoin de communications quotidiennes, une fraternité nouvelle, une pente à l'épanchement, à la manifestation, une curiosité et une impatience d'apprendre, mêlant les individus aux individus, et avec la gazette, qui devient le journal, qui de chronique passe pouvoir, et de passe-temps de pain même de la France, les cafés grandissent et se font *clubs*; leurs tables sont tribunes, leurs habitués orateurs, leurs bruits motions. L'été pluvieux de 1789 fait les cafés pleins. Les cafés... deviennent la presse parlée de la révolution. Les cafés ont un drapeau; et l'on juge de l'opinion d'un homme à Paris par le café dont il est l'habitué. ... La milice nationale, dans tout l'attrait de sa nouveauté, tenant le Parisien hors de chez lui, et le faisant son maître pendant de grands jours, contribue encore à cette vogue et à cette fortune des cafés.[4]

In the Napoleonic period, the massive number of officers and officials in the capital further stimulated the growth of cafés, a growth that the restoration of the monarchy in 1815 in no way restrained. As during the Revolution, the café continued to represent a point of convergence for the innumerable vectors of Parisian life: politics (many cafés still catered exclusively for royalist or liberal patrons); business (the Café Tortoni, founded in 1798, was described by Joseph Mainzer in the 1840s as 'une véritable succursale de la Bourse');[5] journalism and literature, the theatre ('chaque théâtre a son café, qui est, pour ainsi dire, sa succursale,' wrote Mainzer), and so on. Other attractions prompted more and more men (particularly, as we shall see, middle-class men) to favour the café as a social milieu. Not only could newspapers (which until the mid 1830s were available by subscription only) be read there, but a wide variety of games were available; in particular, said Mainzer, 'il n'y a pas de café sans billard; c'est un meuble indispensable. On en compte jusqu'à cinq dans un même établissement, et chacun a sa salle, ses joueurs et sa galerie'.[6] Finally, the rise of the café is linked, both as cause and effect, to the increasing vogue for smoking which, in its turn, is linked to political and social change; 'en général,' wrote Montigny in 1826, 'on fumait très peu chez nous avant que toutes les classes indistinctement fussent appelées à porter les armes,'[7] while the anonymous authors of *Paris-Fumeur* (1855) state that 'le véritable triomphe du tabac en France date de 1830'.[8] All this suggests that, unlike the cafés of the revolutionary period, cafés under the Restoration and the Bourgeois Monarchy were predominantly, even exclusively, male institutions, in contrast to the *salons* of the aristocracy which naturally involved both sexes.[9] As Jean-Paul Aron has suggested in the case of restaurants, it is as though 'au moment même où s'impose l'ordre bourgeois et où s'affirment ses valeurs: respectabilité de la maison, intégrité de la famille, douceur de l'intimité domestique, la société française se ménage des échappatoires'.[10] A product and manifestation of so many social forces, the café paradoxically expresses the triumph of the tightly-knit nuclear family of the bourgeoisie, so different from the looser and more 'porous' family structures of the aristocracy; it is the refuge of the middle-class man from the world of women and children.

The cafés of the first half of the nineteenth century were, Jeanne Gaillard has written, 'des lieux renfermés, un peu secrets, où l'on se retrouve entre soi' and, unlike the extroverted, 'street-oriented' cafés of the Second Empire, 'renferment la clientèle au lieu de la montrer'.[11] In the absence of wide *trottoirs* except on the inner boulevards, most cafés did not possess a *terrasse* and interior comfort (even, in some cases, opulence) went along with relatively undemonstrative exteriors; the aim, it would seem, was to heighten the comfort of regular patrons (the *habitués*) rather than to attract the passer-by (the *casuel*) as it would be in the second half of the century. Some cafés such as the Mille-Colonnes in the Palais-Royal — which, according to Caillot, 'excite l'admiration par le nombre et le volume de ses glaces, dans lesquelles il se multiplie à l'infini'[12] — point forward to the ostentatious designs of the Second Empire, but otherwise the early nineteenth century café, with the primacy it accords to 'inner' rather than 'outer' values, is an image not merely of the bourgeois household but of the 'traditional' bourgeois world-view as a whole. As far as the personnel of cafés was concerned, a particular importance attached to the *dame de comptoir* who was rapidly institutionalized and whose most famous (and original) incarnation was 'la belle limonadière' (Mme Romain) of the Café des Mille Colonnes:

> La dame de comptoir est d'invention toute française. ... C'est sur elle que le cafetier français se repose du soin d'achalander sa maison; lorsqu'il s'agit de la choisir, aucun scrupule ne l'arrête; que ce soit sa maîtresse, sa femme, sa fille, ou une étrangère, peu lui importe: l'essentiel est qu'elle

soit jolie, qu'elle sache écouter avec complaisance les propos galants de l'habitué, et y répondre avec grâce et coquetterie. On l'assied, belle et parée, sur un trône de reine, un divan de velours rouge et vert, surmonté de glaces et de dorures. On place devant elle un roman ou un livre-journal, et à chacun de ses côtés un porte-liqueurs chargé de carafes et de petits verres. Vingt garçons frisés, chaussés d'escarpins, et qu'on prendrait pour des pages, s'agitent autour d'elle, vont et viennent au moindre signal de sa sonnette, comme des esclaves autour de leur sultane.[13]

Most cafés were family affairs and, according to Auguste Ricard writing in 1840, 'on est assez généralement garçon de café de père en fils'.[14] This, together with the primacy, in both numbers and status, of *habitués* over *casuels*, suggests that the pre-1850 café was a closed, intimate institution, characterized by regular contacts between like-minded familiars, in marked contrast to the more open, 'anomic' structures of the *cafés des grands boulevards* of the Second Empire and beyond.

As Maurice Agulhon has shown in his important study *Le Cercle dans la France bourgeoise 1810-1848*, the café is inseparable from that essential institution of pre-1850 bourgeois culture, the *cercle*. Indeed, the *cercle* is often no more than the formalization of the shared intellectual political or commercial interests of the *habitués* of a given café;[15] with its regular meetings (often in the private room of a café), democratic constitution and supply of food, drink and newspapers, the *cercle* was the bourgeois form of 'sociability' *par excellence,* a matrix of political, social and intellectual consciousness as fundamental for the middle-classes as the *salon* was for the old aristocracy. The political and social oppositions of the Restoration and Bourgeois Monarchy may in part be understood, Agulhon suggests, as the opposition between café and *salon*:

> Alors que le salon et le cercle forment un couple antithétique, le cercle et le café sont — bien au contraire les éléments différenciés d'une même réalité globale.... Le cafe-cercle, l'association horizontale-égalitaire, tend à gauche, le salon mondain, l'association verticale-hiérarchique, tend à droite.

Furthermore, organized politics were often no more than an extension of the informal or semi-formal associations of the *café-cercle*:

> Quant à la politique organisée, ce n'en est encore rien d'autre que l'établissement d'une liaison entre ces 'sociétés', 'cercles', 'réunions', groupes d'habitués de cafés, etc. ... Un parti (avant la lettre) ne groupe pas des hommes individuels mais des cercles. Longtemps encore, l'organisation politique empruntera ainsi ses structures à la sociabilité coutumière.[17]

The café marks the translation into the public realm of activities that under the *ancien régime* had normally been conducted in private. Far from being an indicator of the loosening of social ties under the impact of urbanization, the café testifies rather to the intensity of structured or semi-structured interpersonal relations in 'le vieux Paris'. Not only was pre-1850 Paris a complex cellular structure of relatively autonomous *quartiers*, but within each *quartier* there existed a multiplicity of micro-communities — cafés, *cercles* and, as we shall see, *goguettes* and *marchands de vin*, not to mention the *cabinets de lecture*, masonic lodges, *sociétés de secours mutuel* and *corps de garde* that I cannot treat here[18] — all of which contributed to the high degree of personalization of life in the city and made of it, in Michelet's memorable description, 'la capitale de la sociabilité humaine'.[19]

Chapter 4
The Restaurant

The rise of the restaurant parallels that of the café, though in its case the link with the Revolution — which created both the 'supply' and the 'demand' for public eating places — was even more direct. The flight of their aristocratic employers left many *chefs de cuisine* without means of livelihood, while the arrival in Paris of a mass of unattached but comparatively wealthy provincials — officers, officials and administrators for the most part — created a demand for services that the displaced *chefs* were all too pleased to provide. As in the case of the café, the crucial transition is from the private to the public domain; before the Revolution, Maurice Agulhon has written, gastronomy was 'réservée aux Grands dans leurs hôtels *particuliers*' whereas afterwards 'elle se fait accessible aux riches en des commerces *publics*'.[1] The vogue for restaurants continued to grow throughout the Empire and Restoration periods and, significantly, it was during these years that the first and most important gastronomic writings — those of Grimod de la Reynière and Brillat-Savarin — were published: 'à l'extrême fin du VIIIe siècle, la cuisine devient l'objet d'un discours' (Jean-Paul Aron),[2] a sure sign that the pleasures of 'la bonne chère' were being sought and cultivated by a new public composed, in large part, of the 'new men' born of the Revolution and its aftermath. Like the café, the restaurant rapidly became an integral part of the economic, social, political and cultural life or the capital; 'affaires d'intérêt particulier, affaires d'amour, affaires de commerce, affaires d'état, tout se décide à table aujourd'hui,' wrote Montigny in 1825,[3] while in 1827 Antoine Caillot addressed the *restaurateurs* of Paris in the following encomiastic terms:

> Restaurateurs, vous ne savez pas tout ce que vous valez. Apprenez à connaître toute votre importance dans la société. Avec vos déjeuners, vous êtes les régulateurs de l'opinion, des finances, des intérêts des familles, des votes de l'Institut, et quelquefois peut-être de ceux de la Chambre élective. Vous assurez le triomphe des auteurs, et augmentez, par votre influence sur l'art dramatique, les plaisirs de la scène. Dans notre belle France tout roule sur vos tables et autour de vos bouteilles.[4]

According to Caillot, there were 3000 *restaurateurs* and *traiteurs* in the capital in the mid 1820s, catering for 60,000 people daily; the number, he says, rises to over 100,000 if one includes the people who eat at *gargotiers* and *marchands de vin traiteurs*.⁵ This figure clearly reflects the number of unattached males of all classes in the city, and Auguste Luchet, for example, establishes a direct link between the rise of the public eating place and the fact that 'à Paris près de deux cent mille personnes se trouvent isolées chaque jour, sans ménage, sans famille, et quelquefois même sans amis'. ⁶ In contrast to the tightly knit structure of the café, the restaurant appears to bear witness to a loosening of social ties and to the existence in the capital of a large 'floating population' of, in all likelihood, provincial origin.

It goes without saying that restaurants were highly stratified in class terms and that no lower- or even lower middle-class Parisian would even contemplate — let alone be able to afford — eating at Véry's, Vefour's or the Rocher de Cancale. In an interesting aside in *Le Cousin Pons*, Balzac observes that

> les gens du peuple ont peur des officiers ministériels comme ils ont peur des restaurants fashionables. Ils s'adressent à des gens d'affaires comme ils vont boire au cabaret. Le plain-pied est la loi générale des différentes sphères sociales.⁷

Although public eating places were patronized by all classes, it was the bourgeoisie — first its wealthy élite, then its middling strata and, by the 1850s, even the *petite bourgeoisie* — for whom the visit to restaurant became a form of collective rite and for whom eating and drinking in general appeared, in Aron's words, as a 'valeur de prestige' and 'signe de sa promotion sociale'. Writing in his *Almanach des gourmands* (1804), Grimod de la Reynière had no doubt that gastronomy owed 'ses progrès rapides et sa mobile activité' to events since 1789 and to 'le bouleversement opéré dans les fortunes par une suite nécessaire de la Révolution'.⁹ The idea is developed at greater length in his *Manuel des amphitryons* of 1808:

> Dès que l'abondance eut commencé à renaître, les grands artistes en cuisine osèrent se remontrer. ... L'ordre ayant reparu avec un gouvernement stable et modéré, on ne craignait plus de mettre en évidence sa fortune et même de s'en faire honneur ... ; et comme il n'y a pas de moyen plus honorable d'en jouir, que de donner à manger, on vit les cuisines s'échauffer, les tables se relever, et les portes s'ouvrir aux convives, qui jeûnaient depuis tant d'années. Mais, d'un côté, cette longue interruption dans l'exercice des fonctions gourmandes, de l'autre, cette révolution opérée dans les fortunes, qui, en les faisant presque toutes changer de mains, avait mis les nouvelles richesses à la disposition d'hommes étrangers jusqu'ici à l'art d'en user et d'en jouir noblement,

durent apporter un changement presque total dans les mœurs des Amphitryons et dans celles des convives. C'était bien à peu près les mêmes devoirs à exercer, mais ce n'était plus les mêmes individus qui devaient les remplir.[10]

It is difficult to chart the stages whereby restaurant-going was diffused throughout the middling and lower sections of the bourgeoisie. Clearly, a cult of good food had long been customary *within* the middle-class household itself — in 1840 Balzac wrote of the typical *rentier* that 'il s'occupe réellement et sérieusement de sa table, le manger est sa grande affaire'[11] — but the point at which this private passion 'went public' cannot be determined with any precision. All one can say is that, on the evidence of *Paris-Restaurant* (1854), 'eating out' was regularly practised by all sections of the Parisian bourgeoisie in the early 1850s:

> Il est certain que jamais le public parisien n'a dîné plus volontiers hors de chez lui qu'à présent. Le repas de ménage est abandonné de jour en jour. On tend à sortir du petit cercle intime et mesquin. Tous les dimanches et jours de fête, sous le moindre prétexte, on licencie sa cuisinière, on lui donne congé jusqu'au soir.[12]

If, as Jean-Paul Aron claims, 'la cuisine du XIXe siècle est l'histoire de la bourgeoisie et de la possessivité de Paris',[13] the move from private to public eating mirrors exactly the passage from 'introversion' to 'extroversion' that I have indicated in the case of dress and the design of cafés and of which further instances will be noted when I come to discuss shops, the omnibus and the boulevards themselves. A recurring pattern is beginning to emerge: as the bourgeoisie became more sure of tself, it was more and more inclined to display itself and its wealth in public and in the process transformed the structures and institutions of urban life in the light of its new orientation.

Chapter 5
Guinguettes, Goguettes and *marchands de vin*

Immediately after the construction, in the 1780s, of the customs wall (the *mur d'octroi* or *mur des Fermiers-Généraux*) along the perimeter of the present *boulevards extérieurs*, there sprang up directly outside the *barrières* where alcohol was cheaper a profusion of what were known as *guinguettes*: establishments large and small where working-class and lower middle-class Parisians would throng in their thousands every Sunday to eat, drink and dance. There were important concentrations of *guinguettes* at the *barrières* of Montparnasse, Clichy, Montmartre, Rochechouart, La Chapelle, La Villette and Ménilmontant, but the most popular centre was the *barrière de Belleville* and its extension La Courtille (now the Rue de Belleville) which contained the *Bal de la Veilleuse*, the *Folies-Belleville*, the *Ile de l'Amour* and *La Grande Chaumière*; one writer described how, every Sunday in the 1830s and 1840s, 'depuis l'entrée du faubourg du Temple jusqu'au plateau de Belleville, on pouvait voir une véritable marée montante d'ouvriers, de bourgeois, de commis, de grisettes, de bonnes d'enfants et de tourlourous qui tous riaient, chantonnaient, caquetaient et coquetaient à qui mieux mieux'.[1] By the 1820s, *guinguettes* had become big business, as the account given by Antoine Caillot reveals:

> Il est presque impossible de compter les guinguettes qui se sont établies, autour des barrières, à un seul kilomètre de rayon. Réunies, elles formeraient une ville du troisième ordre, d'environ quarante mille habitants. Comme il s'en élève chaque jour de nouvelles, on peut prévoir que dans dix ans elles seront plus nombreuses de moitié. Telle est l'activité des capitalistes, entrepreneurs, propriétaires, que de vastes terrains incultes, escarpés, ou creusés en précipices, ont été nivelés ou comblés pour recevoir de grands édifices, accompagnés de jardins, plantés d'acacias ou de tilleuls. Plusieurs de ces bâtiments, semblables à des palais, attestent le progrès de ce genre de luxe.[2]

Although almost all accounts mention the presence of lower middle-class and even middle-class Parisians at the *guinguettes*, it was without doubt 'le peuple' who were their principal patrons and who gave them their utterly distinctive character. For lower-class Parisians, the Sunday trip to the *barrières* (followed by 'le Saint-Lundi' spent 'sleeping it off', for, as Montigny remarked, 'le lundi est le dimanche des ouvriers')[3] symbolized a rejection of the world of work and the associated values of order, restraint and economy that dominated bourgeois consciousness and which they themselves had to some extent internalized. For many, Sunday at the *barrières* represented, as it were, 'sacred' time devoted to the dissipation of energies and resources accumulated during the 'profane' work-days preceding; 'ces jours-là,' wrote James Rousseau in 1835 of Sunday and Monday, 'on ne peut se faire une idée, quand on n'y a pas assisté, du tumulte qui règne à la barrière pendant douze heures, depuis midi jusqu'à minuit. C'est là que le peuple trouve son plaisir, son délassement, son bonheur, il s'impose des privations toute la semaine pour aller le dimanche à la barrière'.[4] For many middle-class observers such as the 'Hermite de la Chaussée-d'Antin', this systematic flouting of (bourgeois) norms of economy and restraint was a sign of the deep-seated improvidence and fecklessness of the lower classes:

> De temps immémorial, le dimanche est pour eux consacré à dépenser le superflu qu'ils ont pris sur le nécessaire du reste de la semaine. Leur prévoyance ne s'étend pas au-delà de huit jours, et ils ne connaissent d'autre avenir que le dimanche.[5]

At the same time, the role of the *guinguettes* and the cheap liquor they purveyed as a means of releasing, deflecting and neutralizing popular discontents was recognized by conservatives and radicals alike. 'Une révolution venant par le peuple, sans meneurs cachés, ne sera jamais à craindre tant qu'on ne fermera pas les barrières,' wrote James Rousseau,[6] while Martin Nadaud later gave the following bitter account of the effects of the weekly 'binge' on working-class morale:

> Comme les chansonniers des guinguettes avaient poétisé les scènes de la Courtille, il en résultait que chaque dimanche, la jeunesse de l'intérieur de Paris, qui travaillait en chambre, privée d'air pendant la semaine, y accourait en foule, où elle passait la nuit dans des bals éhontés et souvent crapuleux. Les lundis matins, des milliers de femmes échevelées et sans pudeur descendaient dans Paris au bras de leurs cavaliers en état d'ivresse, se culbutant les uns sur les autres narguant le public, lui adressant des propos orduriers. ... Pour les amateurs de spectacles scandaleux et ignobles, l'ensemble de tout ce monde de débraillés et de pochards était curieux et magnifique à contempler. La police ne faisait rien pour prévenir le débordement de ces orgies au milieu de Paris. Mais, on le sait, rabaisser l'esprit du peuple, le dégrader, l'avilir a toujours été pour les gouvernements monarchiques le moyen qui leur a suffi pour perpétuer leur domination et leur empire.[7]

Inevitably, *guinguettes* and *barrières* provided a major focus for prostitution, particularly in the south of the city. In *Les Vierges folles* (1840), Alphonse Esquiros stated that 'on ne rencontre nulle part hors barrière plus de filles qu'à Vaugirard'; living and working in 'cabanes misérablement recouvertes de tuiles et bâties de mœllons unis avec de la terre ... , ces bandes de filles insoumises s'étendent sur la grande ligne des boulevards extérieurs qui commencent à la barrière d'Italie et finissent à celle de Grenelle; elles tiennent, comme on voit, presque toute la rive gauche de la Seine'.[8] At each of the *barrières*, then, there grew up a kind of city in miniature — what Alain Faure in his fine study of carnival in nineteenth century Paris has called 'une ville à l'envers'[9] — devoted to food, drink, dancing and sex and catering for between thirty and fifty thousand Parisians every weekend.

The 'taboo' quality of the *barrières* and the immediate extramural areas — already present, at least in the minds of middle-class Parisians, in their links with drink and illicit sex — was heightened in the early nineteenth century by a further set of associations. They were, in the first instance, doubly related to the world of death. In the late eighteenth century, the cemeteries located within the city precincts had been precipitately closed and demolished: the Cimetière des Innocents (located in the immediate vicinity of the central Halles) in 1780, those of Saint-Roch, Saint-Joseph and Saint-Sulpice in 1781 and that on the Ile Saint Louis in 1782. The dead who had previously, so to speak, cohabited with the living were now physically segregated and banished to new cemeteries outside the official city limits at Vaugirard, Montmartre, Clamart and, above all, Ménilmontant where the Cimetière de l'Est, invariably known as Père-Lachaise, was inaugurated in 1804.[10] In a comparable movement, executions which traditionally had been carried out in full daylight on the Place de Grève in the centre of the city were transferred to the *barrière Saint-Jacques* where they took place — more or less 'en tapinois', as Hugo stated — at dawn.[11] Other 'taboo' activities were systematically shifted from centre to periphery. The slaughter of animals, for example, was no longer carried out by individual butchers on their own premises but was transferred to abattoirs established between 1807 and 1812 on the outskirts of the city; the final concentration of all slaughtering activities at La Villette during the Second Empire completed this process of purification-by-segregation. Immediately outside the *barrières* were located the city's rubbish dumps and cesspools, particularly the notorious Montfaucon to the north east, while striking workers customarily foregathered in the same 'amphibious' extra-mural area — a limbo-landscape, neither city nor country —

so brilliantly evoked by Hugo in *Les Misérables*; finally, the *barrières* — and particularly those of La Courtille, Combat and Ménilmontant — were notorious haunts for criminals as were, a little further out, the abandoned quarries of Montmartre, Montrouge and the Buttes-Chaumont. In a whole number of ways, therefore, the *barrières* were a negation of the spiritual, moral and political values on which the city was based, and it is as though, in a movement analogous to the 'grand renfermement' of the insane described by Michel Foucault,[13] the *polis* was seeking to banish literally beyond the pale those of its aspects and activities that were felt to be unseemly, unsightly or morally obnoxious: heavy industry, cemeteries, rubbish-dumps and cesspools, executions, drink, prostitution and crime. In part (or at least in intention), the structure of early nineteenth century Paris corresponds to the opposition between a 'sacred' or 'pure' centre and 'profane' or 'impure' circumference that Roger Caillois, Joseph Rykwert and others have described in the case of pre-modern settlements and cities.[14] There is, however, one crucial difference. The 'sacred' buildings of pre-1850 Paris — Notre-Dame, the Louvre, the Hôtel de Ville and the Palais de Justice — were indeed located at the centre of the city, and there was indeed a growing tendency to relegate, wherever possible, negative aspects of the city's life to the periphery. But it was precisely at the centre, too, that the most sordid, crime-ridden and insanitary areas of the city were to be found, most notably on the Ile de la Cité itself and amongst the teeming slums and rookeries on the Right Bank opposite. 'Pure' and 'impure', 'positive' and 'negative' were so inextricably commingled in 'le vieux Paris' that, as readers of Baudelaire's 'Le Cygne' will know, one of the most squalid slum areas in the whole city was actually situated *between* the Louvre and the Palais des Tuileries on the present Place du Carrousel,[15] while the criminal haunts described in *Les Mystères de Paris* were located in the immediate vicinity of Notre-Dame and the Hôtel de Ville. In this perspective, the transformation of the city during the Second Empire may be seen as a (largely successful) attempt to disentangle 'pure' and 'impure' and to restore the ideal structural opposition of a 'sacred' centre and 'profane' circumference.

All this underlines what Alain Faure has described as the 'caractère marginal des plaisirs du peuple dans la société bourgeoise'.[16] For weekday drinking, lower-class Parisians frequented the *marchands de vin* which were to be found in every *quartier* of the city. The *marchand de vin* (also known as *cabaret*) was, however, much more than a simple drinking-place; in terms of the formation of social and political consciousness and as an expression of 'sociability', it was essentially the lower-class equivalent of the middle-class café. A whole series of social activities gravitated around the *marchand de vin*: the hiring of workers often took place there, meetings of *sociétés de secours mutuel* or strike committees were commonly held either in the bar itself or in an adjoining room hired for the occasion, the owner was frequently responsible for running saving schemes to which *habitués* contributed and, on a less formal level, workers (and, according to Montigny, others as well) met there in order to read newspapers and other publications:

> Beaucoup d'honnêtes artisans, et même un assez grand nombre de bourgeois aisés et de particuliers des classes immédiatement supérieures, se réunissent en société d'une douzaine de personnes, pour boire chaque matin la demi-bouteille de vin blanc, et lire à haute voix le journal auquel ils sont abonnés en commun. Le nombre de ces réunions tout à fait inoffensives est très grand à Paris; le rendez-vous est établi chez un marchand de vin du voisinage des habitués.[17]

Similarly, Martin Nadaud recalled in his memoirs how, as a boy of fifteen or sixteen, 'tous les matins on me demandait dans la salle du marchand de vin, de lire à haute voix le *Populaire* de Cabet'.[18] According to Auguste Cochin (writing, it is true, in the early 1860s), the services available at many *marchands de vin* were still more diversified:

> Les petits cabaretiers dans les quartiers populaires souslouent généralement un coin de leur boutique à un repasseur de couteaux, un savetier ou, suivant la saison, à une écaillière, une bouquetière, un marchand de marrons ... On y mange sur une table de bois ou de marbre du pain, du fromage, des œufs, de la viande rôtie ou de la charcuterie, du foie sauté, etc ... Ce repas y est toujours subordonné à la consommation de vin. Quelques-uns de ces marchands disposent d'une salle de bal où l'on danse le dimanche.[19]

Cochin further stresses the importance of the *cabaret* in workers' lives at a time when other social ties were beginning to lose their cohesiveness:

> [L'ouvrier n'est] en relation suivie ni avec le patron, ni avec les écoles, ni avec l'Eglise, ni avec les autorités, ni avec les gens de son pays natal, ni avec ses camarades, ni avec une demeure qu'il aime, ni pour ainsi dire avec sa femme et ses enfants. Le cabaret constitue donc le seul lieu de rendez-vous, le cabaret, devenu café-concert, salle brillante, avec mille bougies et vingt billards, attrait bien puissant sur un homme qui va retrouver à la fin d'une journée des enfants qui crient et une femme qui se plaint.[20]

This was the situation in the early 1860s when, as Cochin indicates, the *cabaret*, in common with so much else in Second Empire Paris, had evolved from an 'introverted' into an 'extroverted' institution; in the first half of the century, however, everything suggests that the *marchand de vin* was both physically intimate and, in social terms, often a continuation and intensification of associations formed in the *atelier* or on the *chantier*.[21] Workers from the same *atelier* commonly frequented the same *marchand de vin*, often, it seems clear, in the company of their employer when, as was likely to be the case, a small productive unit was involved; not only this, but *atelier*, *marchand de vin* and home would, in the vast majority of cases, be located close to each other and would represent differentiated aspects of a single social cell. Like the café, the *marchand de vin* constituted a 'knowable' community in which, in most cases, the *habitués* related to each other as whole human beings rather than on the 'segmental' basis which the Wirthian school of sociology holds to be characteristic of urban relationships *as such*.[22]

The Parisian *cabaret* was often, like its Lillois counterpart discussed by Pierre Pierrard, 'la cellule d'un socialisme clandestin'[23] and, as such, was subject to close police surveillance and, not infrequently, to infiltration by spies and informers; the *marchand de vin* himself was often an open or covert radical, though it was certainly not unknown for him to be an *indicateur* instead.[24] The connection between the *cabaret* and political radicalism was such that, less than a month after the *coup d'état* of December 1851, Louis Napoleon promulgated a decree which enabled the police to close down any *cabaret* or drinking-place deemed to threaten public security.[25] Equally suspect to the police and still more cohesively organized were the *goguettes* of which, according to L.A. Berthaud writing in *Les Français peints par eux-mêmes*, there were some three hundred in Paris in the 1840s.[26] Goguettes originated in the early years of the Restoration and were already thriving by the mid 1820s when Montigny described them as follows:

> On compte à Paris une foule de sociétés bien plus bachiques que lyriques, et qu'on désigne par le nom de *goguettes*. Chacune de ces goguettes a son président, son maître de cérémonies et son trésorier; la salle d'un marchand de vin en détail est le lieu des séances, qui se tiennent particulièrement le lundi.[27]

Goguettiers gave themselves agreeably fantastic names such as *Les Braillards, Les Poissons de l'Hippocrène, Les Palefreniers du Cheval d'Apollon* and *Les Enfants du Sans-Souci* and in all that they did displayed a marked sense of corporate identity. A meeting took the form of individual and collective singing, sustained, of course, by much wine and conviviality; a sympathetic observer such as Berthaud stresses, however, that 'ce que le goguettier cherche, ce n'est pas le vin, c'est la compagnie; le vin qu'il boit est mauvais, les gens qu'il fréquente sont bons'.[28] Berthaud goes on to describe a typical session as follows:

> La physionomie des goguettes est partout la même ou à peu près. ... Le président ouvre la séance par un toast et les convives boivent avec lui. ... On chante ensuite, chacun à son tour, et les refrains en chœur. Immédiatement après chaque chanson, le président de la goguette se lève, nomme à haute voix et l'auteur et le chanteur, et invite les goguettiers à applaudir, ce qu'ils font toujours avec beaucoup d'effusion. Un nouveau *toast* est porté au moment de clore la séance, "à l'espoir de se revoir dans huit jours", et tout est dit. Chacun se lève alors et rentre chez soi.[29]

The content of the songs — which, as Berthaud suggests, were often composed by the *goguettiers* themselves as well as performed by them — was often anodine, but even in the mid 1820s Montigny noted that 'la politique n'a pas épargné les goguettes' and that, in consequence, 'la police veut être instruite non seulement de ce qui se fait, mais aussi de ce qui se dit et se chante'.[30] *Goguettes*, indeed, became steadily more politicized as time went on without, of course, ever losing their original 'bacchic' character. In the early 1840s, Berthaud wrote that 'depuis quelque temps surtout, le jeune goguettier semble avoir pris à tâche la glorification du travail et la propagation des idées humanitaires les plus récentes; on dirait un apôtre prêchant son évangile, et c'est un apôtre en effet'.[31] In addition, *goguettes* frequently developed into *de facto* mutual aid societies with members 'clubbing together' to help those of their number who had fallen upon hard times, thus underlining their crucial role in the formation of the social and political consciousness of the Parisian working classes before 1850. Not only did *goguettes* bring together workers of different professions — no mean achievement given the high degree of division of labour in Paris and the many inter-occupational rivalries — but it was also customary for them to pay regular 'courtesy visits' to each other, as a result of which a network of intra- and inter-*quartier* contacts and associations could be built up. As forms of republican-socialist 'consciousness-raising' their impact must have been considerable, not least in the fact that, while professional radical songwriters and performers such as Vinçard *aîné*, Pierre Dupont and Charles Gille existed, many of the songs performed were clearly composed 'by the people for the people'. Just as bourgeois political parties were, as Agulhon has stressed, essentially based on the *café-cercle*, so, it would seem, many of the clubs of 1848 were in the first instance extensions of the associates of the *cabaret* and *goguette*. Once more the lived experience of the Parisian before 1850 proves to be anything but 'anomic' or 'impersonal' in character.

Chapter 6
Shops and Shopping

All descriptions of early nineteenth century Paris stress the enormous increase in the number of shops since the Revolution, an increase that became still more marked after 1815.[1] In 1804 Grimod de la Reynière wrote of 'la métamorphose qui s'est opérée dans les rues de Paris depuis treize ans' and for which, in his view, the increase in the number of shops particularly of food shops — and the evolution of shop design — the greater emphasis on the *étalage*— were largely responsible; as a result of these changes, Paris, he said, appeared as 'une ville absolument nouvelle'.[2] In 1825 Montigny noted that

> partout on a transformé en boutiques, qu'on loue à des taux très élevés, le rez-de-chaussée des plus belles maisons, et jusqu'à celui des hôtels. ... Il suit de là que le nombre des marchands est maintenant presque incalculable; on ne saurait prévoir où s'arrêtera l'espèce de fureur, de fièvre marchande qui s'est emparée de toutes les classes, ni calculer les conséquences fâcheuses qui peuvent en être le résultat. Le plus petit emplacement, le moindre réduit donnant sur une rue, est bientôt disposé en boutique.[3]

The increase in the number of regular shops, together, no doubt, with their greater economic rationality, put pressure on the temporary or semi-permanent *baraques* or *échoppes* which, in the eighteenth century, had successfully coexisted with larger establishments. In 1845 Balzac stated that 'la boutique a tué jusqu'aux éventaires, elle a reçu dans ses flancs dispendieux et la marchande de marée, et le revendeur, et les débitants d'issue, et les fruitiers et les travailleurs en vieux, et les bouquinistes, et le monde entier des petits métiers'.[4] The *échoppiers* resisted tenacement, but were finally destroyed by the *grands boulevards* of the Second Empire, as Charles Vincent lamented in 1867:

> A peine si l'on trouverait aujourd'hui cinq cents échoppes dans cet immense Paris qui, voilà quinze ans, les comptait par milliers. ... C'est que les larges voies font les chers loyers, et que les chers loyers appellent des magasins luxueux qui repoussent les voisinages misérables. ... Les squares élégants ont chassé ces abris populaires. Il faut bien le reconnaître, ces débris du passé font tache à côté des splendeurs du présent. Dans ce Paris nouveau que l'on veut propre et luisant, tout conspire donc contre l'échoppe: aussi les échoppiers disparaissent-ils peu à peu de la voie publique dont ils étaient la vivante gaieté.[5]

Completed under the Second Empire, this process had clearly begun much earlier; the growing extroversion of the bourgeoisie and its reorientation, dating from the mid 1830s, from the interior to the street necessitated, as we shall see in greater detail later on, the removal or, at least, the reduction of the traditional street population of 'le vieux Paris'.

At the same time as shops increased prodigiously in number, so their structure underwent a fundamental evolution.[6] The traditional shop of which *La Maison du chat qui pelote* in Balzac's eponymous novel may be considered typical — was dark, enclosed and introverted; apart from its conventional sign, its exterior would reveal very little about its purpose, and the display of goods for sale was unusual. But, beginning with the restoration of political and economic order in the mid 1790s, 'les marchands,' in Grimod de la Reynière's words, 'renchérissent à l'envi l'un sur l'autre pour donner la plus grande extension au luxe des étalages, absolument inconnu autrefois'.[7] On the basis of the frequency with which the various 'descriptions de la ville de Paris' draw attention to them, these 'tentateurs étalages' must have had an immediate and far-reaching impact on Parisians. Montigny commented that 'l'arrangement des marchandises de la montre est fait avec un goût, une recherche, un tact, une connaissance de l'harmonie des couleurs qu'on ne retrouve en aucun autre pays'.[8] Antoine Caillot was similarly impressed:

> Quoi de plus brillant que la boutique d'un charcutier! au dehors, représentations peintes d'une charcuterie diversifiée de cent manières; verres ou glaces de grande dimension, qui permettent à l'œil de parcourir tous les objets qui s'y vendent; balances d'argent ou de plaqué; charcutière jolie et d'une propreté recherchée sur sa personne; glace derrière elle et banquette de velours d'Utrecht sur laquelle elle est assise. Voyez la boutique de la rue Montesquieu, et admirez. S'il existe encore des boutiques de boulangers et de marchands de vin sans apparence, dans les quartiers habités par le bas peuple, presque toutes celles des autres quartiers se distinguent par des devantures en fer luisant, dont plusieurs ont coûté depuis quatre mille francs, jusqu'à vingt mille, en menuiserie, serrurerie, dorure et peinture.[9]

César Birotteau first sees his wife-to-be in the *magasin de nouveautés* where she works, *Le Petit Matelot* on the Ile Saint-Louis which Balzac describes as 'le premier des magasins qui depuis se sont établis dans Paris avec plus ou moins d'enseignes peintes, banderoles flottantes, montres pleines de châles en balançoire, cravates arrangées comme des châteaux de cartes, et mille autres séductions commerciales, prix fixes, bandelettes, affiches, illusions et effets d'optique portés à un tel degré de perfectionnement que les devantures de boutiques sont devenues des poèmes commerciaux'.[10] In contrast to the 'inner-directed' shops of the past, everything, Balzac wrote in *Gaudissart II* (1844), was now geared towards attracting and pleasing 'l'organe le plus avide et le plus blasé qui se soit développé chez l'homme depuis la société romaine, et dont l'exigence est devenue sans bornes, grâce aux efforts de la civilisation la plus raffinée. Cet organe, c'est *l'œil des Parisiens* ...'[11]

As the structure of shops became more extroverted, with everything calculated to highlight the goods for sale, so the nature and the function of the shop sign changed significantly. Previously, when shops were self-enclosed and otherwise indistinguishable from each other, it was essential that their signs clearly indicated their function, either through some unambiguous conventional *motif* or, as Mercier described, by established a direct link between 'signifier' and 'signified': 'L'enseigne est la chose même; on voit des langues fourrées, des jambons couronnés de laitier, de grasses poulardes, des pâtés vermeils, des gâteaux sucrés qui sont sur le devant; on dirait qu'il n'y a qu'à y porter la main'.[12] Such signs obviously did not disappear but, from the early nineteenth century onwards, there was a growing tendency for shop signs to be geared, like everything else, simply towards attracting the eye of the passer-by rather than towards conveying specific information about the shop in question. In their *Nouveau tableau de Paris* of 1827, for example, Paris and Beauregard commented that 'à présent c'est surtout dans les pièces de théâtre et dans les romans que l'on puise des sujets d'enseigne: ce n'est pas seulement une figure, une personne que l'on expose, c'est une scène tout entière'.[13] This divorce of signifier and signified not only in shop signs but in their exteriors as a whole, became increasingly marked as the century wore on. Writing in 1853 but referring to a Paris that was barely beginning to be 'Haussmannized'. Touchard Lafosse described how

> les capricieuses arabesques, les découpures délicates de la renaissance courent sur la façade de la plupart des constructions qui s'achèvent; le portrait du roi-chevalier est sculpté devant la maison dont un épicier habite le rez-de-chaussée; des études du palais Pitti sont fourvoyées au-dessus d'un magasin de bonneterie; on parvient dans le hangar d'un roulage par un portique décoré d'élégants caissons; et de magnifiques pilastres d'ordre composite se prélassent à la porte d'un apothicaire, qui insulte leur ambitieuse architecture d'une annonce de la pâte Regnault et du taffetas Leperdriel. La marchande de modes fait dorer son balcon, le marchand de vin sa grille; et l'infortuné prolétaire qui veut acheter une

livre de pain hésite à pénétrer dans la boulangerie-boudoir dont l'orgueilleuse entrée se couronne de feuilles d'acanthes.[14]

In much the same way, Maxime du Camp pointed to what he called the 'hypertrophie du langage' which, after the revolution of 1830, led Parisian shopkeepers (and others) to give themselves, their occupations and their establishments such highfalutin names that, it seemed to him, 'les mots ont changé de valeur, et le sens, modifié au cours des générations qui se succèdent, finira par être méconnaissable':

> Autrefois une boutique était une boutique, maintenant c'est un magasin; le marchand est devenu un négociant, le comptoir un bureau, le garçon un commis, la pratique un client; tous les apothicaires sont aujourd'hui des pharmaciens, et quoiqu'il n'existe pas une seule conciergerie particulière, il n'y a que des concierges, et l'on ne trouve plus un seul portier; les perruquiers se sont haussés au rang de coiffeurs; l'un d'eux a été plus loin, et son enseigne nous apprend qu'il est 'artiste capillaire'.[15]

Many of the structural features that are normally associated with the *grands magasins* of the Second Empire — the *vitrine*, the use of lighting and mirrors, the transformation of the shop-front into a highly decorative and eyecatching facade — are clearly present in the shops of the Restoration and the Bourgeois Monarchy. To some extent, too, the process of economic rationalization — the introduction of bulk buying, the bringing together under one roof of many different 'departments', and so on — that would later produce the *grand magasin* had already begun well before 1850.[16] Already *magasins de nouveautés* such as the *Petite Nanette*, the *Magasin des Magots*, the *Vestale*, the *Page Inconstant* and the *Lampe Merveilleuse* (all of them founded in the late eighteenth or early nineteenth centuries) were selling materials of all kinds, and *La Belle Jardinière*, founded in 1824 by Pierre Parissot, may be regarded as the first true *grand magasin* in the city.[17] At the same time, sales techniques became at once more sophisticated and more aggressive; 'savoir vendre, pouvoir vendre, et vendre' was, as Balzac said, the motto of every *boutiquier* in Paris.[18] There was widespread use of advertising, first in the form of prospectuses such as that issued by César Birotteau in order to publicize his *double pâte des sultanes* and *eau carminative* and then, from the mid 1830s onwards, of press advertisements. Just as the owners of cafés used the *dame de comptoir* as a means of increasing their trade, so *boutiquiers* resorted increasingly to attractive shop assistants (both male and female) to boost their sales. In *Gaudissart II*, Balzac describes how the *commis* accosts female customers 'à la façon d'un *deus ex machina*', engulfing them in an atmosphere 'de bonhomie, de jeunesse, de gracieusetés, de sourires, de plaisanteries, de ce que l'Humanité civilisée offre de plus simple, de décevant, le tout arrangé par nuances pour tous les goûts', and many writers stress the role of what, in the same work, Balzac describes as 'les piquantes physionomies et les toilettes des jeunes filles qui doivent attirer les acheteurs'.[19] This 'sexualization' and 'theatricalization' of commerce — whereby the *demoiselle de magasin* became a virtual analogue of the actress and the prostitute — was to be pushed still further during the Second Empire but, once again, the decisive change occurs in the pre-1850 period.

Apart from the general reorientation of shops towards the street, the most important innovation in retailing in pre-1850 Paris was the *passage* or *galerie*. Some *passages* — notably the *Passage des Panoramas* and the *Passage du Caire* — date from the late eighteenth century, while others — for example, the *Galérie Véro-Dodat* (1822), the *Passage de l'Opéra* (1823) and the *Galerie Vivienne* (1823) — are products of the Restoration period; still others, such as the *Passage Jouffroy* (1845), were established under the Bourgeois Monarchy. Many of these *passages* were located in the increasingly middle-class west of the city and owed their success to the concentration of shops they permitted and their seclusion from the turmoil and squalor of the Paris streets. Nonetheless, there were *passages* in other parts of the city, and a clear class differentiation pertained here as elsewhere. The *Passage de l'Opéra* in the west of the city was characterized, wrote Amédée Kermel in *Le Livre des cent-et-un* (1833), by 'une allure de bonne compagnie que vous trouverez peu ou point dans les autres passages de la capitale' whereas the *Galerie Vivienne* close to the Palais-Royal constituted 'le chaînon qui joint aux boulevards un des quartiers les plus industrieux de la ville'. There was, Kermel continued, a clear contrast 'dans les régions de l'industrie et de la bourgeoisie':

> Les passages Vendôme, Bourg-l'Abbé, Saucède, et tous ceux compris dans ce rayon, représentent la classe positive dans notre société. L'habitué d'un de ces obscurs bazars se trouvera presque dépaysé au passage de l'Opéra; il lui tardera d'en sortir.

Finally, said Kermel, nothing was 'plus attristant que l'aspect du passage Brady, où la misère et la malpropreté semblent avoir établi leur quartier-général; c'est un bazar à friperies, et pas autre chose'. Despite this class differentiation, the bourgeoisie was disappointed in its desire to segregate itself from other classes if, as Kermel claims, some of the most opulent *passages* soon became a haunt for criminals and other undesirables:

Dans les passages avoisinant les quartiers de la Bourse et de la Chaussée d'Antin, quartiers envahis depuis longtemps par l'aristocratie de l'argent, on peut remarquer un air d'aisance et de luxe qui va décroissant à mesure qu'on s'en éloigne, et comme l'or est la puissance aimantée qui attire à elle tout ce qu'il y a d'existences douteuses et de consciences vénales, c'est là que circulent les impuretés sociales de la grande ville; filous, femmes entretenues, débauchés de corps et d'esprit, filles de joie, mendiants à gages ou exerçant par goût pour le *far niente* des lazzaroni: en un mot, le vol, le vice et la fraude sous tous les masques, sous tous les costumes.[20]

According to Jeanne Gaillard, the *passages* are typical of the 'structures urbaines fermées' of the first half of the nineteenth century in that they 'renferment la vie publique de la belle société au lieu de l'extérioriser.' and permit 'une pratique quasi confidentielle de la vie commerciale'. Furthermore, the *passages* constituted yet another series of 'micro-cells' within the broader cellular structure of the *quartier*; they were, wrote Texier in 1853, 'autant de petites cités mercantiles ou industrielles' in which 'les gens qui les habitent ... se connaissent tous, et cultivent avec le plus grand succès la chronique scandaleuse'.[22] While the *passages* as such were introverted and quasi-autonomous, the shops that composed them were, as Caillot's description of the *Galérie Véro-Dodat* indicates, structurally and humanly extroverted in a manner that once more points forward to the *grands magasins* of the Second Empire:

> [La Galérie Véro-Dodat] est infiniment remarquable et digne de toute la curiosité des nationaux et des étrangers. Sur une longueur d'environ trente toises, [elle] offre de chaque côté dix-huit boutiques, dont l'extérieur est orné de pilastres, de baguettes de cuivre doré, de grands verres qui laissent une entrée libre à toute la lumière du jour, et entre lesquelles des glaces de toute hauteur, et d'une largeur médiocre, donnent aux passants la facilité de s'y considérer depuis les pieds jusqu'à la tête. L'intérieur de ces boutiques répond à l'éclat de leur dehors: toutes parfaitement éclairées par le gaz hydrogène, ainsi qu'un grand nombre d'autres de la rive droite de la Seine, elles ne cachent rien de ce qui peut exciter les désirs des acheteurs, dont le nombre augmente de jour en jour par l'accroissement de la population parisienne.[23]

Even under the Restoration and the Bourgeois Monarchy, then, what Touchard Lafosse later called 'le *négociantisme*' had already begun to encompass Paris 'de ses bras de Briarée'.[24] Older commercial practices were, of course, by no means totally superseded. For every *Magasin des Magots* there would long be a dozen *Maison-du-chat-qui-pelote* and for decades yet *échoppes* would struggle to survive alongside the newer *boutiques*; at many popular shopping-places, such as the second-hand clothes 'bazaar' on the Rue du Temple, shopkeepers, as the hero and heroine of *Les Mystères de Paris* find to their delight, continued to approach potential customers in a way that was 'à la fois empressée, prévenante et joyeuse', but, Suë comments pointedly, 'ces façons, empreintes d'une sorte de familiarité respectueuse, semblaient appartenir à un autre âge'.[25] The future clearly belonged to the *passages*, the *magasins de nouveautés* and the *grands magasins*, establishments where economic rationality, the introduction of fixed prices, the use of a whole range of 'hard sell' techniques and the single-minded pursuit of profit were rapidly leading to a reification of the relationship between buyer and seller. At the same time and as part of the same process. the entire physical structure of shops was turned ostentatiously outwards in order to attract, inveigle, provoke and frustrate the passer-by. With luxury that had previously been concealed now put arrogantly on display, poorer Parisians became painfully and angrily conscious of the increasingly blatant distance between themselves and 'les oisifs'. More and more, lower-class Parisians were impotent spectators of the wealth of others, endlessly confronted by *vitrines* packed with goods they could not hope to acquire. The image of the Parisienne before the *vitrine* of a *magasin de nouveautés* is more than just a *topos* of sentimental, *bien-pensant* or utopian socialist literature. It expresses a reality of class relationships that will lead directly to the head-on confrontations of June 1848:

> Aux carreaux d'un magasin à prix fixe: les étoffes en tout genre roulent, ruissellent et bouillonnent à l'étalage ..., tout cela chiffré, numéroté au grand rabais, rien n'a été oublié pour allumer les imaginations féminines, dénaturer l'innocence d'un jeune cœur et y implanter les désirs, l'envie, l'ambition. ... Elle soupire et mesure d'un œil désespéré la distance sociale qui sépare son tablier de serge noir et son cabas de ces points d'Angleterre, de ces mantilles encadrées de fourrure.[26]

Chapter 7
The Omnibus

Until 1828 when the first omnibuses were introduced, no collective form of public transport existed in Paris, movement about the city being assured by privately owned *carrosses* and *cabriolets* (about 10,000 in number in 1826) supported by approximately 2000 *voitures de place* available for individual private hire. According to Delphine de Girardin, the form of privately owned carriages underwent a significant evolution in the late 1830s as, along with so much else, they became structurally more extroverted and individualized, aiming to display and no longer to conceal their passengers:

> Toutes les voitures se ressemblaient à Paris; elles avaient la même forme et la même couleur, elles étaient toutes régulièrement laides, lourdes et de mauvais goût. Aujourd'hui, les calèches légères, les briskas, les cabriolets à quatre roues et même à six roues ont remplacé les grandes berlines dites de famille, et les *landaus* massifs, dont la trappe entr'ouverte ne vous laissait apercevoir que le bleu du ciel et menaçait toujours de vous engloutir en se refermant sur vous.[1]

But it was the introduction of the omnibus that made the deepest and most immediate impact on Parisian life. Bearing exotic/erotic names such as *Carolines*, *Sylphides*, *Dames Françaises*, *Joséphines* and *Algériennes* (a further instance, perhaps, of the growing 'sexualization' of urban life), the omnibuses ran on fixed routes and at regular times and charged relatively low fares (initially 0.25 francs per journey). After some resistance from individual forms of public transport, by the early 1830s the omnibuses were by far the most popular way of moving around the city and were patronized by members of all classes, including, according to one contemporary, the Duchesse de Berry who 'accompagnée d'une ou de deux dames affectionnait beaucoup ces voitures, et prenait grand plaisir à se promener incognito'.[2] It was, however, the middling sections of the bourgeoisie who were the principal beneficiaries of the omnibus whose increasing popularity, like that of the restaurant and the café, signified, in Maurice Agulhon's words, 'la mise, par le commerce, à la disposition de la classe moyenne d'une pratique sociale (rouler en ville en voiture) qu'une mince élite accaparait naguère sous la forme privée de la voiture de maître'.[3]

The omnibus, wrote Edmond Texier in 1853, was 'la démocratisation du véhicule',[4] a sentiment echoed the following year by the anonymous authors of *Paris-en-omnibus* when they stated that 'l'omnibus est un agent de progrès démocratique; l'omnibus rapproche les distances, confond toutes les classes de la société, mêle tous les rangs'.[5] Nonetheless, in bringing together members of different classes in a state of unwonted physical proximity, the omnibus served only to reveal the growing economic, social and psychological distances between them. In the first place, as Victor Fournel wrote in 1879, the shifting population of the omnibus as it moved from east to west graphically illustrated the class polarization of the city:

> Les omnibus ont leurs habitués et leur population flottante. La physionomie des habitués varie naturellement selon les lignes. Telle ligne est plébéienne, telle autre bourgeoise; une troisième presque aristocrate, autant que peut l'être une ligne d'omnibus. La plupart offrent des nuances et se mélangent d'éléments nouveaux, suivant les quartiers qu'elles traversent, et aussi suivant les heures du jour. Presque toutes sont prolétaires à huit heures du matin et s'embourgeoisent dans l'après-midi. L'omnibus qui va de la Bastille à la Madeleine, peuplé surtout d'ouvriers et d'ouvrières à son point de départ, change de couleur à mesure qu'il avance, comme un courant qui se modifie d'après les rivières qu'il reçoit et les pays qu'il traverse. Passé le boulevard du Temple, les bonnets sont en minorité, et après la porte Saint-Denis, les chapeaux ronds et les bottines vernies submergent les casquettes et les souliers à clous.[6]

Secondly, the closed world of the omnibus was the very antithesis of the various 'micro-communities' that we have discussed in the previous pages. Here more than anywhere else in the city Parisians were objects to each other; contacts, such as they were, were fleeting and 'segmental' in character and, in general, the omnibus furnished an image of a thoroughly atomized and divided society. 'Rien ne porte à la tristesse et la mélancolie comme de voyager souvent en omnibus,' wrote the authors of *Paris-en-omnibus*:

> L'habitué d'omnibus, à quelque sexe qu'il appartienne, est un être sombre, silencieux, concentré en lui-même. L'omnibus rend farouche et misanthrope. ... On s'assoit à côté les uns des autres sans rien dire; les femmes abaissent leur voile, les hommes ramènent leur chapeau sur leurs yeux. Si un voyageur fait arrêter la voiture, on se serre en rechignant pour qu'il prenne sa place.[7]

The omnibus was, in Texier's words, a 'théâtre ambulant' in which the passengers were 'spectateurs les uns des autres', anxiously—or amusedly — sizing up their neighbours, as eager to penetrate the inner lives of others as they were to conceal their own.[8] Horace Raïsson (beneath which name Balzac may be lurking pseudonymously) went still further:

> L'omnibus est une espèce de cimetière, où tous les rangs, toutes les conditions, tous les états sont confondus; on se prend, on s'enchâsse, on se quitte sans un salut, sans un mot, sans un geste; on paye, on acquitte sa place, et c'est tout. L'omnibus est un symbole du siècle où nous vivons; le *suum cuique* est gravé sur tous les fronts: l'égoïsme, l'impertinence, l'égalité, mais cette égalité dans les manières et dans la mise, que l'on prend par habitude, qu'on quitte par orgueil, sont sculptés sur tous les panneaux, se reflètent sur tous les visages. C'est l'arche de Noé, c'est un paradis commun, c'est un husting ambulant, c'est un lupanar, c'est tout ce qu'on veut, tout, excepté une voiture.[9]

The omnibus, in short, embodied a shifting, 'anomic' society in which one-dimensional beings — 'une série de silhouettes,' as the Goncourt brothers say in their remarkable description of an omnibus journey in *Manette Salomon* (1867)[10] — enter into brief and usually uneasy pseudo-relationships with each other. Perhaps it was because of the multiple tensions generated by the confined space within the omnibus itself that the *impériale* became increasingly popular from the early 1840s onwards. Whatever the reason, the authors of *Paris-en-omnibus* had no doubt that 'les voyageurs de l'impériale deviennent chaque jour plus nombreux. une grande révolution est en train de s'opérer dans nos habitudes. ... l'impériale est un des besoins les plus impérieux de l'époque'.[11] Once more an extroverted structure was beginning to displace one that was inner-directed.

Chapter 8
Bals publics

Although public dance halls had existed in the eighteenth century, it was once again in the first half of the nineteenth century that saw their transformation into a central institution of Parisian life. The range and variety of *bals publics* mirror the extraordinary heterogeneity of the city's population itself with its myriad divisions, sub-divisions and sub-sub-divisions; as Alain Faure has written, 'chaque public a son bal, comme chaque bal son public'.[1] Texier describes the bewildering variety of public dance halls as follows:

> Nul ne pourrait poursuivre jusque dans ses dernières limites l'énumération des bals et lieux quelconques où on se livre à la danse: il faudrait écrire un livre spécial, et encore! Il y a des salles de bal où l'on n'est admis qu'en blouse! d'autres où la bourrée règne sans partage, et où le contrôle fait subir un interrogatoire dans l'idiome le plus pur du Cantal ou de l'Aveyron. Telle enceinte ne reçoit que des messieurs en livrée et leurs dames; telle autre n'ouvre sa porte qu'aux casques des pompiers. ... Les chiffonniers, par droit de conquête, se sont réservé d'inabordables sanctuaires à la barrière du Maine; les gens de maison expulseraient impitoyablement tout intrus qui pénétrerait dans leur *Salon de Mars*.[2]

It is likely that a majority of those present at such provincial or professional gatherings would have been known to each other on at least some basis and that once more one is in the presence of the 'cellular' structure so characteristic of 'le vieux Paris'. Nonetheless, small *bals* of this kind are of decidedly lesser importance than the massive (often open-air) dance halls that began to appear after 1815 and reached their apogee under the Bourgeois Monarchy, dance halls such as the *Bal Mabille*, the *Bal Musard*, the *Ranelagh*, the *Prado*, the *Bal Chicard*, *La Chaumière*, the *Closerie des Lilas* and the *Bal des Variétés*. Larger *bals* were to be found in most parts of the city, but were particularly numerous around the *barrières* to the north and the north-east; a number catered for the student population of the Latin Quarter, and the Champs-Elysées contained several open-air establishments, notably the celebrated *Bal Mabille*. All *bals publics* charged entrance fees and openly competed with each other for custom. Publicity was widely employed, patrons were solicited by all manner of attractions — fireworks, *montagnes russes*, games, lighting effects and so on — and many *bals* hired professional *danseurs* and, particularly, *danseuses*, at least two of whom, Rigolboche and Mogador, rapidly attained to the status of 'living legends'. Like the *guinguettes* (from which in certain respects they cannot be wholly differentiated), the larger *bals publics* were frequented by Parisians of all classes, but it was undoubtedly 'le peuple', in the broad early nineteenth century sense of the term, that gave them their distinctive character, and if members of other classes ventured there, as they certainly did, it was only on condition that they conformed to the *mores* of the popular majority. In 1835 the Austrian ambassador, Count Apponyi, described the *Bal des Variétés* as follows:

> Il faut voir là le peuple parisien dans toute sa gloire, avec une liberté entière, sans surveillance de police, car il n'en souffrirait pas dans l'intérieur de la salle; c'est son domaine, tout doit se régler d'après lui, il est despote; il veut non seulement ne pas se gêner, mais il veut que tout le monde soit comme lui, qu'on adopte ses vêtements, ses manières. Pour lui plaire, il faut sinon devenir son égal, du moins tâcher de l'imiter, sans quoi on risque d'être traité de mouchard ou d'aristocrate, dans les deux cas on ne s'en trouverait pas bien.[3]

Despite this popular *dominante*, rigid social stratification or segregation do not appear to have obtained in the larger *bals publics* of the first half of the century. According to Taxile Delord's account in *Les Francais peints par eux-mêmes*, the *Bal Chicard* presented 'le plus curieux pêle-mêle de nuances sociales' and the *chicard* himself could be indifferently 'étudiant, dandy ou clerc de notaire, commis ou négociant de peaux de lapins': 'Là, plus de numéro d'ordre, plus de catégories, de conditions; tout est nivelé, fondu dans l'immense tourbillon des costumes et des quadrilles'. On the other hand, the *Bal Chicard* was certainly not an anonymous congeries of individuals but presented a definite structure and sense of corporate identity; according, once more, to Delord, 'n'est pas admis qui veut dans ce bal qui a son genre d'aristocratie, ou de franc-maçonnerie, si l'on aime mieux. ... Le bal Chicard a ses rites, ses règlements, ses préceptes qu'il faut connaître d'avance, sous peine de se voir excommunié et voué à Musard. C'est une cérémonie religieuse, un culte, une adoration'.[4] How far other *bals* conformed to this pattern cannot be stated with precision, though the comments of the Prince de Joinville on the *Variétés* in 1841 suggests that the *Bal Chicard* was by no means exceptional: 'Pas un habit noir dans la salle. Tout le monde, hommes et femmes costumés, tout le monde se connaissant. Et quelle gaieté, quel entrain'.[5] Certainly, for Victor Rozier, writing in 1855, it was clear that the *bals* of even the early years of the Second Empire — let alone the huge barns that Huysmans, Taine and the Goncourts would later evoke — were markedly less 'personal' than their Bourgeois Monarchy equivalents: 'presque tous les bals, jadis, avaient un cachet particulier qu'on ne retrouve plus aujourd'hui'.[6] In the opinion of contemporaries, there had never been dancing as frenetic, orgiastic and excessive as under the Restoration and, still more, under the Bourgeois Monarchy. All commentators were agreed that the *chahut* and the *galop*, the two most popular dances of the pre-1850 period, differed from earlier dances in a manner that most found disturbing and repugnant. According to Louis Véron, it was in the aftermath of the July revolution that

> la jeunesse des écoles et le peuple se plurent, de concert, à la singulière fantaisie de révolutionner la danse française; ils remplacèrent les mouvements arrondis, élégants, lentement développés de l'ancienne gavotte de nos pères, par une danse frénétique, convulsive, irrespectueuse, indécente, qu'on appelait d'un mot approprié à la chose, le *chahut*. On fit même un verbe, *chahuter*.[7]

The *chahut* was danced with a partner and seems, on the basis of Taxile Delord's account, to have given great scope to individual improvisation and expression, at once erotic, salacious and satirical in intent. It was, says Delord, not merely a 'parodie de la volupté' but 'une parodie de l'amour, de la grâce, de l'ancienne politesse française':

> Ici les figures sont remplacées par des scènes; on ne danse pas, on agit; le drame de l'amour est représenté dans toutes ses péripéties; tout ce qui peut contribuer à en faire deviner le dénouement est mis en œuvre; pour aider à la vérité de sa pantomime, le danseur, ou plutot l'acteur, appelle ses muscles à son secours; il s'agite, il se disloque, il trépigne, tous ses mouvements ont un sens, toutes ses contorsions sont des emblèmes.[8]

The *galop* was even more 'dionysiac' for here formal partners were abandoned and the participants swirled together in search of collective delirium in a 'tourbillon immense qui entraînait et faisait tourner avec lui tout ce qu'il accrochait au passage'.[9] The *galop* as practised at the *Bal Musard* was particularly notorious, as the following account by Delphine de Girardin demonstrates:

> Quant au quartier du centre de Paris, il ne valse ni ne danse, il ne saute ni ne croule; il tourne, il roule, il tombe, il se rue, il se précipite, il s'abîme, il tourbillonne, il fond comme une armée, il vous enveloppe comme une

trombe, il vous entraîne comme une avalanche ... c'est l'enfer qui se déchaîne, ce sont les démons en congé, c'est Charenton qui jouit de la vie ..., c'est une apparition un jour de fièvre, c'est un cauchemar, c'est le sabbat, c'est enfin un plaisir terrible qu'on nomme le *galop de Musard.*[10]

It was, wrote Privat d'Anglemont, as though the whole city had been seized by 'le pêle-mêle étourdissant de la danse sans frein et sans forme'.[11] What was the meaning of this mass quest for ecstasy which, popular in origin, seemingly held the young of all classes in its grip?

Many commentators adopted a simple-minded moralistic approach, but the more perceptive linked the emergence of the *chahut* and *galop* to a whole complex of political and social circumstances. Véron saw the orgiastic dances of the Bourgeois Monarchy as one symptom amongst others of the 'profonde commotion' caused by the July revolution which had raised extravagant hopes amongst the lower classes and in the student milieu only to crush them forthwith beneath the dead weight of the *juste-milieu* and its rallying cry, *Enrichissez-vous!* After 1830, said Véron, 'les cœurs furent lents à se calmer, les esprits à se rasseoir, les intérêts à reprendre confiance; le sans-gêne, le *débraillé*, s'introduisirent dans les costumes, dans les mœurs et jusque dans le langage'; in this perspective, the *chahut* and the *galop* offered release to energies and passions that could find no outlet in constructive political and social action.[12] Other commentators, too, saw the dances as symptoms of disillusion and frustration. For Delord, they recounted 'l'histoire de notre scepticisme',[13] while in his despatch of 7th February 1842 to the *Gazette d'Augsburg* Heine proposed a searching political interpretation of the whole phenomenon of the *bal public*:

> Il me semble parfois qu'on y bafoue en dansant tout ce qui est regardé comme noble et sacré dans la vie des hommes, mais ce qui a été si souvent exploité par des fourbes et rendu ridicule par des imbéciles, que le peuple ne saurait plus y croire comme autrefois. ... Les fanfaronnades de l'impuissance surtout ont tant dégoûté ce peuple de toutes les choses idéales, qu'il n'y voit plus rien autre que des phrases vides de sens, que de la *blague*, comme il dit dans son argot.[14]

Not only the lower classes and the student population but also, according to Delphine de Girardin, the sons of the aristocracy sought release from their frustration with the Bourgeois Monarchy in the *galop* and the *chahut*. 'Les bals Musard et Valentino ont toujours la vogue,' she wrote in 1838,

Le bal Musard est déjà une vieille folie consacrée par le temps et adoptée par l'usage. Les jeunes gens de la meilleure compagnie, les héritiers de nos plus grands noms, y vont dépenser l'ardente activité que l'*émigration intérieure* et leurs répugnances politiques leur laissent toutes entières; ils dansent, ils galopent, ils valsent avec enthousiasme, comme ils se battraient si nous avions la guerre. ... Ils ne vont pas aux fêtes de la cour, fi donc! ils y trouveraient leurs notaires et leurs banquiers; mais ils vont chez Musard: là, du moins, ils trouvent leurs valets de chambre et leurs palefreniers; à la bonne heure! On peut, sans se compromettre, danser en face de ces gens-là.[15]

In the opinion of contemporaries, then, the *chahut* and the *galop* expressed not merely the alienation of the lower classes after 1830 but also the disaffection of what Balzac described in *Un Prince de la Bohême* (1840) as 'la fleur inutile, et qui se dessèche, de cette admirable jeunesse française que Napoléon et Louis XIV recherchaient, que néglige depuis trente ans la gérontocracie sous laquelle tout se flétrit en France'; it was, Balzac continued, young men whose careers were blocked and hopes frustrated who, at carnival time, 'déchargent le trop-plein de leur esprit, à l'étroit durant le reste de l'année, en des inventions plus ou moins drôlatiques'.[16] In short, the *galop* and the *chahut* are, no less than *Lorenzaccio*, *Lucien Leuwen*, Bohemains and *Bousingots*, expressions of that complex and contradictory mood of nihilism, apathy, utopianism and despair that spread to the young of all classes in the aftermath of 1830. Born of the 'dangereux ébranlement' (Louis Véron) of the *trois glorieuses*, the *chahut* and the *galop* point forward to the still greater commotions of February and June 1848.

On the other hand, at least one writer — the unfortunately anonymous author of *Paris-Dansant* (1845) — saw the *bal public* and its dances not as the sign of an approaching crisis but as the matrix from which an alternative social order might be born. Clearly a Fourierist by conviction, the author makes a series of telling contrasts between the cramped individualism of private dances and the heady collectivism that reigns at the *bal public*:

Quand nous le comparons au bal du bourgeois, au bal de l'individu, même dans l'aisance, le bal public qui puise les éléments de son luxe dans la bourse de tous les particuliers, nous fait comprendre par ses verres de couleur, par des globes de gaz, par ses pavillons chinois, par son vif orchestre, la puissance de l'ASSOCIATION, cette fée qui doit transformer le monde.

With 'ces hommes et ces femmes qui se touchent à peine du bout du doigt, qui avancent et reculent en cadence, comme des poupées à ressort', the private dance symbolizes that state of atomistic individualism and psychosomatic frustration which, for the Fourierist, characterizes the present epoch; even 'la musique du bal particulier trahit un effort impuissant de l'individualisme qui s'essoufle en voulant réaliser une œuvre collective'. The *bal public*, on the other hand, symbolizes integration, freedom, creativity:

> On est libre à Mabille, à la Chaumière, à Valentino. Là, chacun danse comme il l'entend; il peut marcher comme dans le grand monde; il peut aussi tricoter des entrechats et faire la roue dans les solos de pastourelle; les dames sont libres de boire et de fumer.

Finally, the *bal public* becomes an image of the co-operative, communalistic society to come:

> Ne parlez donc plus des individualités, du ménage bourgeois pour donner des fêtes! Vive l'association! Associons-nous pour danser, pour valser, pour polker; plus tard nous nous associerons pour la culture, pour l'industrie, pour la cuisine, et les choses n'en iront plus mal.[17]

Whether they were interpreted as symptoms of a deep social and political malaise, as forms of regenerative associationism or as a combination of both, it was clear to contemporaries that the *bals publics* and their frenetic *danses* were linked in some fundamental way to the *physionomie* of the age. As Heine informed the readers of the *Gazette d'Augsburg*: '"Nous dansons ici sur un volcan" — mais nous dansons'.[18]

Chapter 9
Carnival

In his *Paris Carême-prenant* (1978), Alain Faure has argued strongly for the continued vitality of carnival in pre-1850 Paris, seeing it as a time of symbolic classlessness or, more precisely, as the 'temps du peuple roi' in which 'un imaginaire innocent créé par et pour le peuple' reigned supreme.[1] Carnival, he argues, was Sunday at the *barrières* writ large; for its duration, the norms governing 'profane' society — economy, restraint, purposeful and productive activity — were systematically flouted and Parisians of all classes, but particularly 'le peuple', gave themselves up to riotous dancing, laughter, masquerade and the exorbitant consumption of food and drink. Carnival, in this view, was the last vestige of the sacred in an increasingly desacralized city. Individuals and social groups who normally remained uneasily distant from each other briefly fused in Bacchanalian oneness; on the streets 'masqués et non masqués occupaient le même espace, tous étaient de la même fête' so that carnival was a 'living theatre' involving not actors and spectators but 'spectateurs-participants' who, for the time of its duration, deliriously negated all the co-ordinates upon which established society was founded. In the second half of the century, Faure continues, carnival entered into decline but experienced a resurgence of vitality after 1890 as part, perhaps, of what another historian, Michael R. Marrus, has called the 'great collective binge' on which, he claims, the whole of French society embarked in the twenty five or so years before the outbreak of the First World War.[2] After the supreme carnival of February 1848 in which, says Faure, 'Fête et Révolution étaient l'une dans l'autre' and in which 'l'insurgé fut tour à tour charivariseur, barricadier et bouffon',[3] the annual orgy was 'recuperated' by the established order and transformed into a tame fancy-dress parade-cum-commercial gala: 'les seuls [masques] qu'on rencontre maintenant sur les boulevards représentent quelques maisons de commerce,' wrote Victor Rozier in 1855, 'les commis de ces maisons, déguisés en polichinelle et en arlequin, portent sur toutes les coutures les adresses de leurs patrons'.[4] For Faure, the decline of carnival under the Second Empire — when, as Hugo trenchantly observed, 'tout ce qui existe étant un carnaval répandu, il n'y a plus de carnaval'[5] — serves only to throw into still greater relief what he sees as its extraordinary vitality in the first half of the century.

Faure adduces much evidence in support of his view and there can, of course, be no doubt that, compared with the insipidities of the Second Empire, carnival in 'le vieux Paris' was vitality itself. Nonetheless, the causes of its later moribundity must, it seems to me, be sought in the pre-1850 period and not attributed unlilaterally to its commercialization under the Second Empire. Estimates of the vitality of a given year's carnival are notoriously subjective, but what is certain is that at some point during the first half of the nineteenth century carnival in Paris ceased to be primarily an outdoor phenomenon and withdrew physically and metaphorically behind closed doors. Writing in 1853 but clearly referring to a situation that had obtained for some time, Edmond Texier stated aphoristically that 'le carnaval ne court plus la ville; il a cessé d'être nomade et d'égayer les rues par ses caravanes animées, par ses drapeaux flottants et ses costumes aux mille couleurs'. The decline of carnival as a street spectacle is unambiguously recorded by E.J. Delécluze in his diary entry of February 15th, 1825:

> Décidément, le Carnaval se meurt en France. Ces files de voitures fermées qui marchent lentement, toute cette population parée qui sort de chez elle pour jeter un regard méprisant sur le peu de population qui paraît masquée dans les rues, le sérieux glacial qui règne sur tous les visages, tout indique que le temps de carnaval n'est plus une époque de divertissement populaire. On a bien plus l'air de venir s'assurer qu'il y a des masques que pour jouir de leur vue.[7]

On the basis of this account (which Faure does not quote), carnival as early as the mid 1820s did not consist of 'spectateurs-participants' but rather of a clearly demarcated group of actors and an infinitely larger number of spectators, while even in the much more vigorous description of the carnival of 1833 in *Les Misérables*, a definite division obtains between 'revellers' and 'onlookers'. In Hugo's account, too, there is, despite much conviviality, little evidence of a fusing of individuals and still less of a merging of the classes. Everything is strictly regulated by the authorities with the 'défilé ... de véhicules de toutes sortes, fiacres, citadines, tapissières, carrioles, cabriolets, marchant en ordre, rigoureusement rivés les uns aux autres par les règlements de police et comme emboîtés dans des rails' while all the time 'les voitures armoriées des pairs de France et des ambassadeurs tenaient le milieu de la chaussée, allant et venant librement'.[8] The revelries of carnival continued but, crucially, they now took place indoors, at the Bal de l'Opéra (which, after 1836, was open to members of all classes), at *bals publics* and, increasingly, at private festivities; according to the police statistics of 1836, there were 182 public and 874 private dances (excluding the *barrières*) on *Mardi Gras* that year.[9] The dance halls' gain was the street's loss; in February 1837 Delphine de Girardin recorded that there were 'presque point de masques sur les boulevards; tous les travestissements étaient réservés pour les bals de Jullien et des petits théâtres'.[10] Carnival in pre-1850 Paris presents us, then, with a paradox: at a time when traditionally private activities such as eating, drinking and travelling were 'going public', this traditionally street-based, public celebration was subject to increasing privatization. I shall return to this problem in the concluding section of this essay.

Chapter 10
Saltimbanques and Prostitutes

The fate of that other key figure in popular street entertainment, the *saltimbanque*, resembled in many respects that of carnival: police harassment, official regulation and marginalization before 1850, outright repression, expulsion or, in the case of those few who survived, commercialization under the Second Empire. There can be little doubt that during the Restoration period *saltimbanques* could be found in all parts of the city save, perhaps, exclusively *grand bourgeois* or aristocratic 'ghettoes' such as the Chaussée d'Antin and the Faubourg Saint-Germain, with the Boulevard du Temple, that Mecca of popular entertainment in 'le vieux Paris', being, not surprisingly, the choicest terrain for street performers of every kind. Writing in 1863 in the emotional aftermath of the Boulevard's demolition as part of the *Haussmannisation* of Paris, Théodore Faucher described how, in the first quarter of the century, its pavements teemed with

> bateleurs avec leurs baraques en toile et en bois: les uns montrant des lièvres qui battaient de la caisse; des puces qui traînaient des carrosses à six chevaux; les autres faisaient voir des femmes qui pesaient huit cent livres; des hommes qui avalaient des cailloux, des serpents, des fourchettes; des enfants qui buvaient de l'huile bouillante, qui marchaient sur des barres de fer rouge.[1]

The fires of 1826 and 1827 which destroyed the *Cirque Olympique* and the *Ambigu* along with numerous cafés and other buildings led to major reconstruction which, combined with increasingly stringent police supervision of street entertainers and *petits industriels*, significantly changed the character of the whole area. After 1826, wrote Faucher,

> l'aspect du boulevard n'était plus le même. Des maisons avaient été bâties, les petits fossés comblés; les boutiques garnies par des grilles en bois ou en fer, à hauteur d'appui, et les théâtres, ayant des auvents soutenus par des colonnes posées sur le sol, avaient un air de propreté, presque d'élégance, qui n'existait pas avant; leurs devantures étaient pavées ... Plus de saltimbanques, plus de parades ... plus de grosse caisse ... Au bruit avait succédé le calme, peut-être la monotonie ... [2]

For Nerval, writing in 1846, the physical reconstruction of the Boulevard and the new vigilance of the police were but different aspects of the same process of 'normalization':

> Le Boulevard du Temple a perdu toute sa physionomie en s'embellissant, en s'assainissant, en épurant sa société et ses mœurs. La municipalité l'a soumis à l'alignement; la police aux bonnes manières. Il n'a plus ni les bateleurs, ni les danseurs de corde.³

Just as carnival was being driven off the streets into various indoor locations, so sword-swallowers, acrobats, fire-eaters and other street entertainers were exposed to increasing harassment as the authorities sought to take control of the streets and pavements of the capital. As more and more succumbed to that pressure, an essential form of the traditional 'participatory' culture of the people was in danger of extinction:

> En vérité, la joie populaire s'en va: les règlements de police l'ont tuée. Le spectacle des *bagatelles de la porte* n'était-il pas le seul spectacle des pauvres gens, la consolation de leur soirée, l'attrait tout-puissant qui les empêchait de porter leur dernier sou au cabaret?⁴

By the late 1840s, *saltimbanques* along with their close kinsfolk, the *petits industriels* — that infinitely diverse world of knife-grinders, boot-blacks, rat-catchers, chair-menders, itinerant sellers of bootlaces, matches, ribbons, balloons, paper windmills and whatever which, according to Texier, 'commence partout et ne s'arrête nulle part'⁵ — were clearly an endangered urban species, and the rich human comedy of the Paris streets to which they had contributed not merely their trades, skill, artistry and sleight of hand but also their distinctive cries and costumes was, through their demise, itself subject to ever greater semantic impoverishment. In a remarkable passage in *Par les champs et par les grèves* inspired by a visit to Brest during his tour of Britanny in 1847, Flaubert brings together in a single complex meditation many of the archetypal figures and features of 'traditional' urban life on the eve of their extinction:

> Autrefois, lorsqu'on se promenait, on avait chance ... de rencontrer des ours, des bateleurs, des tambours de basque, des singes habillés de rouge, dansant sur le dos d'un dromadaire, mais tout cela est également parti, est également chassé, proscrit sans retour; la guillotine est hors barrière et fonctionne en cachette, les forçats vont en voiture fermée et les processions sort défendues! Dans quelque temps, les saltimbanques aussi auront disparu, pour faire place aux séances magnétiques et aux banquets réformistes, et la danseuse de corde bondissant dans l'air avec sa robe pailletée et son grand balancier sera aussi loin de nous que la bayadère du Gange. De tout ce beau monde coloré, bruissant comme la fantaisie

même, si mélancolique et si sonore, si amer et si folâtre, plein de pathétique intime et d'ironies éclatantes, où la misère était chaude, où la grâce était triste, dernier cri d'un âge perdu, race lointaine qu'on disait venue de l'autre bout de la terre, et qui nous apportait dans le bruit de ses grelots comme la vague souvenance et l'écho mourant des joies idolâtrées, quelque fourgon qui s'en va sur la grande route, ayant des toiles roulées sur son toit et des chiens crottés sous sa caisse, un homme en veste jaune escamotant la muscade dans ses gobelets de fer-blanc, les pauvres marionnettes des Champs-Elysées et les joueurs de guitare des cabarets hors barrière, voilà tout ce qui en reste.[6]

The demise of *saltimbanques*—who, according to Fournel, were 'attachés de cœur aux principes démocratiques qui forment la base de notre immortelle Révolution'[7] — was hastened by their involvement, real or imagined, in the dissemination of radical republican propaganda through mime song and satire. After the repression of the *journées de juin* street performers of all kinds were subject to rigorous police supervision leading in many cases, to eviction and expulsion from their traditional haunts whence the enormous pathos — both human and political — of Daumier's paintings and lithographs of rejected or fugitive clowns executed in the immediate aftermath of the Bonapartist *putsch* of December 1851.[8] With few exceptions those *saltimbanques* who survived the political repression of the 1850s were swept into oblivion in the wake of *Haussmannisation*. In an interesting article published by *La Cloche* in June 1872, Zola describes how, under the Second Empire, the administration, not content with expelling *saltimbanques* from within the old pre-1860, city limits,

a nourri surtout une haine féroce contre les fêtes de la banlieue annexée. Ces fêtes dérangeaient la belle symétrie du gigantesque hôtel garni rêvé par l'Empire. ... Les fêtes populaires gênaient cet idéal. Elles laissaient traîner sur les tapis la loque d'un *saltimbanque*, des mirlitons crevés et des miettes de pains d'épice. L'Empire pudibond baissait les yeux pour ne pas voir la femme colosse. Il sentait une vague raillerie dans les cabrioles et les coups de pied des paillasses. Et il semblait dire que son sentiment élevé de l'art ne pouvait tolérer les orgues de Barbarie, les toiles peintes des cirques forains, la pauvreté des baraques jetées le long des trottoirs dans tous les tohu-bohu du campement. Aussi fit-il une terrible guerre aux fêtes des quartiers excentriques. Il les abolit les unes après les autres, celles de Montmartre, de Belleville, de Montrouge. Il rêva de porter la main sur les grandes foires, la foire aux pains d'épice entre autres, mais le temps lui manqua. D'ailleurs, il traquait les camelots, les saltimbanques, les jeux de toutes sortes. Vers les derniers temps, un marchand forain me disait toutes les amertumes du métier; ils étaient à la merci de la préfecture qui donnait les meilleures places à ses favoris, saisissait les marchandises à la moindre infraction, gouvernait ce peuple des fêtes comme une bande de forçats.

There was, according to Zola, an attempt by the administration 'd'aligner les fêtes et de les rendre dignes de ses boulevards' by constructing standardized booths for the use of officially licensed performers and sideshows. Predictably, they remained empty; 'ces baraques disent tout l'Empire' is Zola's acid comment.[9] By 1876, when Victor Fournel published his *Esquisses et croquis parisiens*, 'le saltimbanque maigre et nerveux d'autrefois, dévoré par le soleil, par la faim, et par l'amour de l'art' had almost completely disappeared to be replaced — insofar as he was replaced at all — by a new breed of professionals, 'gras, fleuris et dodus', who, clad in 'des costumes où les paillons étincellent comme des rayons de soleil', 'font imprimer des affiches, ils distribuent à la foule des prospectus illustrés où le maître de la baraque s'intitule "gérant de l'entreprise"'.[10]

As *saltimbanques* were driven off the larger thoroughfares first into the backstreets, then beyond the *barrières* and finally into virtual extinction, so their place on the streets, squares and boulevards of the capital was taken by prostitutes. In the first half of the nineteenth century, and especially before 1830, it is evident that prostitution in Paris was largely confined to certain clearly defined areas — the Palais-Royal, the Ile de la Cité, the *barrières*, the newly constructed *quartier* around Notre-Dame-de-Lorette — and that, thanks in part to the official policy of marginalization and reclusion, it was far from a city-wide phenomenon and, above all, was by no means ubiquitously visible.[11] Gradually. however, prostitution began to emerge from the semi-visible margins of society to which it had hitherto been largely restricted. The 'regularization' of the Palais-Royal in the late 1820s caused prostitutes to spill over into adjoining *quartiers*, the construction of stations in the 1840s provided them with a new focus for their activities together with an almost limitless supply of customers, and by the 1850s prostitution had spread to such an extent that it was clear to many observers that a whole new phenomenon had emerged. In his preface of 1873 to *Les Vierges folles* (first published in 1840), Alphonse Esquiros emphasized how

> sous le Second Empire la prostitution s'est transformée. Il y eut moins de filles publiques en maison; il y eut beaucoup plus de filles libres. ... On vit se répandre sur nos boulevards, sur nos places et nos promenades, dans

nos cafés et nos établissements publics, une nuée de femmes aux faux cheveux, aux fausses couleurs, étalant au grand soleil ou sous la lumière de gaz tous les oripeaux d'un luxe effronté. Ce n'était plus la prostitution cachée, séquestrée, honteuse d'elle-même. C'était la débauche triomphante et levant partout la tête.[12]

For the first time, the *fille publique* became truly public. Not even the most fashionable and exclusive areas were exempt: 'elles ont envahi les boulevards,' wrote Texier, 'partout, entre le débouché de la Chaussée-d'Antin et la rue d'Angoulême, on les voit circuler, l'œil lascif et aux aguets, la démarche provocante, le sourire stéréotypé sur les lèvres'.[13] Not only did prostitutes stand and walk on the pavements of the new boulevards but they swiftly invaded and made their own the *terrasses* of the equally new boulevards cafés. 'J'aperçois un grand changement dans la prostitution,' reads an entry of January 1864 in the Goncourt diary,

Tout à l'heure, elle était ambulante, vaguante, trottinante, fuyante à l'œil. C'était quelque chose qui vous frôlait, passait, filait. Aujourd'hui, Paris a une prostitution assise, — assise en plein éclat de gaz, aux tables des cafés des boulevards, rangée en ligne, faisant front aux passants, insolente avec le public et familière avec les garçons à tablier blanc.[14]

In the course of this unprecedented movement outwards, the appearance of prostitutes — never, of course, exactly 'introverted' even during their period of relative reclusion — became even more extravagantly 'other-directed'. The process is well described and analyzed by the leading modern authority on prostitution in nineteenth century France:

La rue désencombrée, les terrasses de café qui envahissent la chaussée, l'éclairage au gaz puis à l'électricité permettent à la prostituée de circuler inlassablement, de se donner au besoin des airs de femme du monde, d'entraîner le marcheur dans son sillage bruissant et de s'exhiber. ... La séduction quitte les espaces confinés — boudoir, loge, salon de la maison de tolérance — où le parfum pénétrant de la femme constituait un de ses plus sûrs atouts. Le primat du visuel accompagne le déclin relatif de l'olfaction. On ne respire plus tant le corps alangui; on subit la fascination des formes en mouvement; le désir devient cinétique.

Even the interiors of the new-style brothels — themselves typically more 'open' and 'impersonal' than the *maisons closes* of the earlier period are 'spectacular' and 'extroverted' in their structure:

La grande maison de tolérance, sans abandonner les parfums ventilés, sacrifie surtout à la vue; elle abrite des spectacles, elle se donne des allures de temple grec, de palais vénitien, de sérail turc. Les pensionnaires sont en représentation. La tenancière, devenue metteur en scène, multiplie les glaces et les éclairages électriques que les sexologues du temps accusent de détraquer l'équilibre nerveux du client, candidat au voyeurisme.[15]

'On le croyait d'abord exceptionnel et excentrique à la vie parisienne,' wrote Castagnary of the *demi-monde* in 1866, 'on s'aperçoit maintenant que, dans la vie parisienne, tout, ou presque tout, converge vers lui'. This apotheosis — it is nothing less — of the prostitute in Second Empire Paris and, in particular, her colonization of the public places that had formerly teemed with *saltimbanques, petits industriels* and other highly individualized denizens of 'le vieux Paris', aptly symbolizes the triumph of one 'model' of urban civilization over another. Metaphorical equivalents, Haussmannized city and ubiquitous whore embody the reduction of all values, meanings and values to those of the market, the transformation of human beings into interchangeable units in an all-encompassing and depersonalizing urban system: 'Le grand signe de la fille tombée à la prostitution,' wrote the Goncourt brothers in 1862, 'c'est l'impersonnalité. Elles ne sont plus une personnalité, mais une unité de troupeau. Le *moi* disparaît d'elles, c'est-à-dire la conscience et la propreté de soi'.[17] The 'Babylone de l'avenir', as, once again, the Goncourts described Haussmann's Paris in 1860, was, like the prostitutes it spawned in ever increasing numbers, based on the principle of *étalage*, of the primacy of appearance over substance, of signifier over signified, of outwardness over *innéité*; everything in 'le nouveau Paris' — streets, buildings, people, even the pseudo-nature of parks, squares and promenades — is permanently *en vitrine*.[18] These notions, too, will be developed in the section that follows.

Chapter 11
Conclusion: 'Public' and 'Private' in pre-1850 Paris

What general conclusions can be drawn from this necessarily selective survey of certain of the more institutionalized forms of everyday life in Paris in the first half of the nineteenth century? What do developments in dress, eating and drinking habits, forms of transport and so on tell us about the underlying structure of existence in a city so patently poised between 'old' and 'new'? In the first place, changes in class structure and, linked to them both as cause and effect, the vastly increased importance of money in all aspects of life — are reflected, sometimes immediately and obviously, sometimes indirectly and subtly, in the general contexture of everyday living. In the sixty or so years following the Revolution of 1789 there had occurred, wrote Balzac in 1845, 'une étrange métamorphose sociale' as a result of which 'les trois ordres anciens' had been replaced 'par ce qui s'appelle aujourd'hui des *classes*'; the old ascriptive order had been steadily but remorselessly eroded until finally it succumbed as an organizing principle 'au citoyen, au bourgeois, au prolétaire, à l'industrie et à ses victimes'.[1] Where previously inherited rank had been the primary (though not always the sole) determinant of social position, now money became the principal (though again not always the sole) creator of status. The meaning of the transformation was formulated with admirable concision by Guizot:

> Nous assistons depuis trois quarts de siècle au spectacle de l'insuffisance et de la fragilité de toutes les supériorités que donne le sort, de la naissance, de la richesse, de la tradition, du rang. La conviction que l'homme vaut surtout par lui-même et que de sa valeur personnelle dépend essentiellement sa destinée, c'est là aujourd'hui, dans la société française, un sentiment général et profond.[2]

The 'new society' was one in which all citizens were equal in theory but unequal in fact; not inherited rank, but money as the source and expression of 'valeur personnelle' was now the great differentiator. Towards the end of the Empire, the 'Hermite de la Chaussée-d'Antin' had written that 'la fortune est devenue chez nous la mesure de l'estime que l'on accorde à ceux qui la possèdent',[3] while in *Melmoth réconcilié* Balzac was even more categorical: 'Notre civilisation, depuis 1815, a remplacé le principe Honneur par le principe Argent'.[4] Once legal and theoretical equality was established, it became increasingly urgent to achieve and demonstrate inequality in fact, for, as, again, Balzac wrote in *Ferragus* (1833), 'plus nos lois tendront à une impossible égalité, plus nous nous en écarterons par les mœurs'.[5] The most immediate and important expression of this 'will to inequality' was the westward movement — already well advanced by 1840 and accentuated and accelerated, but emphatically not caused, by *Haussmannisation* — of the Parisian bourgeoisie which contemporary observers were quick to seize upon and which modern historians have analyzed in detail.[6] But the constitution of the bourgeoisie as a class required that its members distinguish themselves by every possible means both from those above them and from those beneath, from which latter group many — perhaps most — of their number had themselves emerged within living memory. Initially, however, their collective self-image (not to mention their immediate economic interests) depended far too closely on the notions of restraint, economy and hard work for them to demonstrate their newly acquired wealth and status through conspicuous consumption; that had been the way of the old aristocracy from whom they were as anxious to differentiate themselves as from the masses below, at least until the mid 1830s. Until their position was thoroughly secure, they distinguished themselves from other classes through private rather than public consumption. The *habit noir* and the modest dress of their wives and daughters indicated clearly to fellow bourgeois and others alike that they were neither of 'le peuple' nor of the aristocracy; as we have seen, all forms of bourgeois dress before 1830, female as well as male, were certainly directed outwards as bearers of a social message, but in a fundamentally unostentatious, even self-effacing, manner. Other forms of bourgeois status assertion were unambiguously private or semi-private in character, directed inwards towards their fellows rather than outwards towards other classes. Individual and collective identity was asserted either in the home itself (the cult of the family, the importance attached to having a 'good table', the attention and expense devoted to interiors rather than exteriors) or in intermediate areas such as the café, the *cercle*, the *corps de garde* and the restaurant which, although public (and to that extent different from the private *salons, manèges* and banqueting halls of the aristocracy), were nonetheless sufficiently enclosed structurally and socially to be virtual surrogates of the home, presenting — at least as far as middle-class men were concerned — an ideal blend of both public and private realms. However, once the aristocracy had been displaced and the threat presented by the lower classes in the years immediately following 1830 had been neutralized — in other words, from about 1835 onwards —, there are unmistake-

CONCLUSION 63

able signs of a movement from 'inwardness' to 'outwardness' on the part of large sections of the now dominant bourgeoisie. While male dress remained unchanged, that of middle-class women became increasingly ostentatious; the design of carriages and of the shops, cafés and restaurants patronized by the bourgeoisie showed a definite tendency towards 'extroversion' and a life-style that had previously been oriented towards the home and towards 'public-private' areas such as the *cercle* now took the public world of street, *boulevard* and *trottoir* as its theatre. Where status had previously been asserted through various forms of 'sociability' with one's fellows, the emphasis was henceforth to be on the public display of wealth in the presence of others. His position secure, the Parisian bourgeois, in the erstwhile manner of the aristocracy he had displaced, would henceforth constitute himself as a spectacle for the Other.

The Paris of the middle classes may be divided, then, into three contiguous but politically, socially and psychologically distinct areas: the private (home), the intermediate (the *café-cercle*, the restaurant and the *passages*) and the public (the boulevard and those activities and institutions that are conceived in function of it). In this perspective, the history of the Parisian bourgeoisie may be interpreted topographically as a progression from the private realm (the *ancien régime*) via 'public-private' forms of sociability and action (the Revolution, Empire, Restoration and early years of the Bourgeois Monarchy) to the public sphere (the second two-thirds of the Bourgeois Monarchy and, following the temporary setback of 1848, the Second Empire). According to Jeanne Gaillard, Paris in the first half of the nineteenth century — I would prefer to say, rather, until the mid to late 1830s — was 'une ville renfermée sur elle-même où la bourgeoisie abandonne la rue au populaire'.[7] No sooner, however, had the bourgeoisie secured its victory of 1830 than it desired to appropriate, even to colonize — the streets and pavements of the city which it felt now belonged to it by right if not yet in fact and began to dream of an urban environment in which it could display itself and its wealth to greater advantage and, above all, in conditions of complete security. Early evidence of this growing bourgeois predilection for 'le dehors' is to be found in an interesting work of the early 1830s, *L'Epoque sans nom, esquisses de Paris 1830–1833*, where the author, M.A. Bazin (the pseudonym, it would seem, of Anaïs de Raucon), speaks of 'cette vie extérieure, ce monde en plein vent, ce commerce de regards, de propos, de compliments échangés au passage, cette sociabilité ambulante' which, she says, 'est surtout ce qui caractérise notre grande ville, et ce qui en fait le principal agrément'. The Parisian — by which she means not merely the middle-class Parisian — is possessed, she says, by a 'continuel besoin de mouvement et de pêle-mêle qui le pousse hors de son logis', a need which, as far as middle-class Parisians are concerned, could be pleasantly and securely satisfied only on the *boulevards intérieurs*, 'cet espace si bien préparé pour nos goûts et nos besoins, enceinte et centre en même temps, communication et point de ralliement, que l'on suit, que l'on traverse, où l'on passe, où l'on va, d'où l'on vient, toutes choses importantes dans notre existence de Parisiens, et qui là se trouvent admirablement réunies'.[8] But the inner boulevards (even, more precisely, their western portion) apart, where else could the middle classes sate their new-found passion for 'le dehors'? Existing streets, squares and (where they existed) pavements were narrow, squalid and — the final horror — teeming with those very lower classes from which the bourgeoisie wished at all costs to distance itself. Despite the westward movement of the bourgeoisie and the parallel but contrary movement of 'le peuple' to the east, the middle-class Parisian of the 1830s and 1840s could still not escape — certainly not in the centre of the city and not always in 'his' territory in the west — the spectacle of the lower classes, that 'peuple horrible à voir, hâve, jaune, tanné' which Balzac describes in the extraordinary opening pages of *La Fille aux yeux d'or* (1834).[9] As he walked through the streets, cane in hand, the Parisian bourgeois was likely to be accosted by beggars, robbed (even, as we have seen, in *passages* close to the Chaussée-d'Antin itself), taunted by mischievous *gamins* and harassed and impeded by the hundreds of *petits industriels, marchands ambulants, échoppiers, saltimbanques* and *charlatans* who infested such pavements as existed. In 1837 Delphine de Girardin complained that

> les rues aujourd'hui sont des bazars où chacun étale ses marchandises, des ateliers où chacun vient exercer au grand jour son état; les trottoirs, déjà si étroits, sont envahis par une exposition permanente. ... Le fait est qu'aujourd'hui le trottoir appartient à tout le monde, excepté à celui qui en est le possesseur naturel, c'est-à-dire le piéton.[11]

But even before 1850 the pedestrian — needless to say, the bourgeois pedestrian — was, with the help of the municipal authorities and the general evolution of society, beginning to get the upper hand. The *échoppe*, as we have seen, was being driven out of business by the *boutiques*, *saltimbanques* were subject to incessant police harassment presaging their final expulsion from the streets during the Second Empire, *petits industriels* of all kinds were being overtaken by economic and technological advances and, according to Balzac writing in 1845, 'charlatans, ces héros

CONCLUSION

de la place publique, font aujourd'hui leurs exercices dans la quatrième page des journaux'.[12] Similarly, carnival, the traditional street-based feast of the people, was being forced indoors, its subversive potential neutralized by privatization and commercial exploitation. The pattern is clear: as the middle classes moved outwards, so the traditional population of the Paris streets was being driven inwards, eastwards or simply forced out of existence in order to make way for them. More and more, working-class Parisians were being made to feel aliens, passive spectators of an ever more theatrical, pseudo-aristocratic and acquisitive bourgeoisie; already in the 1840s Parisian society was splitting into what the Goncourts — at a time (1865) when, of course, the division was still more blatant — would call 'deux classes: [...] les hommes qui se font regarder et ceux qui les regardent'.[13]

Such a division between *regardants* and *regardés* was, to say the least, ominous. In *Choses vues*, Victor Hugo describes a ball given in July 1847 at the Parc des Minimes in the Bois de Vincennes and attended by the *fine fleur* of the Bourgeois Monarchy including Guizot, Thiers, Rothschild, the Prefect of Police, Lord Normanby, Dumas *père* and *fils*, Gautier, Vigny and Hugo himself. In order to reach the ball, guests had to drive eastwards from their western fastnesses through the working-class heartland of the Faubourg Saint-Antoine, with predictably calamitous results:

> Depuis quinze jours on [...] parlait [de la fête], et le peuple de Paris s'en occupait beaucoup. Hier, depuis les Tuileries jusqu'à la barrière de Trône, une triple haie de spectateurs garnissait les quais, la rue et le faubourg Saint-Antoine, pour voir défiler les voitures des invités. A chaque instant, cette foule jetait à ces passants brodés et chamarrés dans leurs carrosses des paroles hargneuses et sombres. C'était comme un nuage de haine autour de cet éblouissement d'un moment. [...] Quand on montre le luxe au peuple dans des jours de disette et de détresse, son esprit [...] franchit tout de suite une foule de degrés; il ne se dit pas que ce luxe le fait vivre, que ce luxe lui est utile, que ce luxe lui est nécessaire. Il se dit qu'il souffre et que voilà des gens qui jouissent; il se demande pourquoi tout n'est pas à lui. [...] Ceci est plein de périls. Quand la foule regarde les riches avec ces yeux-là, ce ne sont pas des pensées qu'il y a dans les cerveaux, ce sont des événements.[14]

Barely six months after M. de Montpensier's ball at the Parc des Monimes, the working-class resentments described by Hugo would indeed erupt in a series of turbulent *événements* which, though we cannot discuss them in detail here, may readily be interpreted as a penultimate attempt by 'le peuple', pending the final reckoning of 1871, to reassert control over the streets of a city which it felt less and less able to call its own. Not only this: all the characteristic actions of radical Republicans in 1848 — the endless delegations and deputations that converged on the Hôtel de Ville, the Palais-Bourbon and the Palais du Luxembourg, the attempt to exert pressure on elected representatives by invading the Assembly in May, the transformation of clubs, the Luxembourg commission and *ateliers nationaux* into would-be 'paragovernments', to use Peter Amann's term[15] — may themselves be seen as, with remarkable perceptiveness, Charles de Rémusat did at the time, as so many attempts to 'dominer le dedans par le dehors',[16] in other words to use the street-based power of 'la foule' to influence, control and finally to overcome the Provisional Government and its successor whose power base lay *within*; in the eyes of radicals, reacting against the growing invisibility of government under the Bourgeois Monarchy, the Republic was to be, first and foremost, a *res publica*. In this perspective, the political history of the Republic from February to June 1848 appears as a progressive triumph for 'le dedans' over 'le dehors'. Carried to power by the streets in February, the Provisional Government, evolving into the Executive Commission, steadily extended its authority over those same streets until, victorious in June, it was able to dominate them entirely. Henceforth, as once again Charles de Rémusat makes amply clear in his memoirs, the middle classes were secure in a city which only now could they truly call their own:

> On voudrait bien peindre la situation de Paris après les journées de Juin. Le sang qui avait à flots rougi les pavés était à peine étanché. Le deuil avait pénétré dans l'intérieur de bien des familles. On en rencontrait à chaque pas les sombres couleurs. ... Et cependant on éprouvait un sentiment de satisfaction qui, si l'on avait osé, serait devenu de la joie. ... On se sentait délivré de la menace d'un joug cent fois plus dur que la loi la plus sévère. Le nuage sombre, qui pesait depuis quatre mois sur notre horizon, était dissipé, ou du moins éclairé. ... Aussi la ville égayée par le temps de la saison offrait-elle un aspect animé, original et presque riant. Le luxe n'avait pas reparu dans les lieux publics, mais le monde s'y montrait comme en des jours de fête. La sécurité et la curiosité se peignaient sur tous les visages.[17]

But still the problem of the streets themselves remained. Marcel Cornu's recreation, in *La Conquête de Paris* (1972), of the state of mind of the Parisian bourgeoisie in the 1840s and, still more, after its triumph of June 1848 cannot, in our view, be bettered:

CONCLUSION

> A mesure que les bourgeois, grands ou petits bourgeois, prennent mieux conscience de leur puissance, de leur rôle dans la société, de leur dignité, ils ont dû se sentir frustrés. En somme, privés de leur droit à Paris. Effectivement ils ne se situent pas ostensiblement dans l'espace de leur ville. Engluée dans ce magma pâteux du centre, la bourgeoisie se distingue insuffisamment des classes inférieures. Ses demeures, ses rues ne signifient pas la place qu'elle a conquise dans la société. Car telle est une des fonctions de la ville. La conformation urbaine tend à refléter la conformation sociale. Le statut d'une classe sociale prépondérante doit pouvoir se lire, à livre ouvert, sur la ville, grâce à la distribution différenciée des espaces et à la qualification des architectures.[18]

As we have seen, the movement of the bourgeoisie out of the centre began rather earlier than Cornu allows, but otherwise his analysis of the middle-class perception of the city is both suggestive and, one cannot but feel, correct. After 1850 the Parisian bourgeoisie began to reoccupy — though not to reinhabit — those areas in the centre and, to some extent, in the east of the city from which they had withdrawn in the course of the previous fifty to seventy years; Haussmann's boulevards were the instrument of that reoccupation. *Haussmannisation* was a complex and multifaceted phenomenon, but fundamentally it was the recreation of Paris by the bourgeoisie for the bourgeoisie and in the bourgeoisie's own image. The boulevards were the means whereby the middle classes took possession physically and psychologically of 'their' city. No text better captures this sense of appropriation, this new feeling of 'at-homeness', than Zola's description in *La Curée* (1872) of the reaction of Renée Saccard and her stepson-lover to the newly *Haussmannised* City:

> Les amants avaient l'amour du nouveau Paris. Ils couraient souvent la ville en voiture, faisaient un détour, pour passer par certains boulevards qu'ils aimaient d'une tendresse personnelle. Les maisons, hautes, à grandes portes sculptées, chargées de balcons, où luisaient, en grandes lettres d'or, des noms, des enseignes, des raisons sociales, les ravissaient. Pendant que le coupé filait, ils suivaient d'un regard ami les bandes grises des trottoirs, larges, interminables, avec leurs bancs, leurs colonnes bariolées, leurs arbres maigres. Cette trouée claire qui allait au bout de l'horizon, se rapetissant et s'ouvrant sur un carré bleuâtre du vide, cette double rangée ininterrompue de grands magasins, où des commis souriaient aux clientes, ces courants de foule piétinant et bourdonnant, les emplissaient peu à peu d'une satisfaction absolue et entière, d'une sensation de perfection dans la vie de la rue. ... Ils roulaient toujours, et il leur semblait que la voiture roulait sur des tapis, le long de cette chaussée droite et sans fin,

qu'on avait faite uniquement pour leur éviter les ruelles noires. Chaque boulevard devenait un couloir de leur hôtel.[19]

Nothing could be clearer. Before, say, 1835 the Parisian bourgeoisie felt truly secure only at home or in home-surrogates such as the *café-cercle*; in the Second Empire, after an intermediate period when its growing desire for 'outwardness' was thwarted by the city's physical and human structure, the boulevards became both its home and the stage upon which lt displayed its wealth, status and power. Henceforth, as Zola suggests and as I have argued in greater detail elsewhere,[20] the whole of bourgeois life is reoriented towards the boulevard. The structure of houses becomes extroverted, geared as much towards impressing the passer-by as securing comfort for its inhabitants; cafés, restaurants and shops are likewise conceived in relation to the boulevard, and in every aspect of existence the principle of *étalage* — with its concomitant divorce of form from substance, of signifiers from their signifieds — supplants the earlier norms of inwardness and concealment. As Alfred Delvau wrote in *Les Dessous de Paris* of 1862: 'Tout le luxe est dehors, — toutes les richesses sont en montre, toutes les séductions sont en étalage. — tous les plaisirs font trottoir'.[21]

But, paradoxically, as life became more public, so individuals became more isolated. As we have seen, not only was 'le vieux Paris' a polynuclear structure of relatively autonomous cells but each cell, each *quartier*, was itself a honeycomb of interlocking micro-cells — cafés, *cercles, ateliers, marchands de vin, goguettes* and so on, not forgetting the *lavoir,* that 'haut-lieu de la sociabilité féminine, qui joue dans la vie du quartier un si grand rôle' (Michelle Perrot)[22] — which sustained individuals in their sense of themselves and, by blending the intimate and the public within a knowable context, created an ideal terrain for the forging of significant links with others. But, under the influence of the same social, economic and political forces that brought about the 'extroversion' of the *quartier* after 1840 or so, many of these micro-structures were themselves distended, loosened or, in some cases, destroyed. The interaction between self and city was no longer — or, rather, was less successfully — mediated through a complex reticulation of 'private-public' institutions and, as Richard Sennett has demonstrated in a work — *The Fall of Public Man* (1976) — to which the present argument is much indebted, 'private' and 'public' came more and more to be seen as antithetical terms.[23] No longer sustained by a tight-meshed network linking self to micro-community to *quartier* to city, the individual tended increasingly to confront Paris

CONCLUSION

as a solitary ego before an undifferentiated, hypo-significant urban mass; in Cochin's terms, he was ceasing to be an active 'citoyen' and was becoming a mere 'habitant', observing rather than participating in the life of the *polis*. Michelet's 'capitale de la sociabilité humaine' was on the wane; the era of the Lonely Crowd had dawned.

Notes and references

Unless otherwise stated, works in English are published in London and those in French in Paris.

Chapter 1: The *flâneur*

1 'Un flâneur', 'Le flâneur à Paris', in *Paris, ou le livre des cent-et-un*, T.6 (Schmerber, Frankfurt, 1832), p.61.
2 Auguste de Lacroix, 'Le flâneur', in *Les Français peints par eux-mêmes*, T.3 (Curmer, 1840), p.66.
3 'Un flâneur', 'Le flâneur à Paris', p.60.
4 de Lacroix, 'Le flâneur', p.66.
5 de Lacroix, 'Le flâneur', p.72.
6 Victor Fournel, *Ce qu'on voit dans les rues de Paris* (Adolphe Delahays, 1858), p.263.
7 Victor Fournel, *Esquisses et croquis parisiens*, 1ere série (Plon, 1876), p.220.
8 'Un flâneur', 'Le flâneur à Paris', p.62.
9 Alfred Delvau, *Les Dessous de Paris* (Poulet Malassis, 1862), p.9.
10 Charles Lenormant, 'Du costume parisien et de son avenir', in *Paris, ou le livre des cent-et-un*, T.7 (Schmerber, Frankfurt, 1832), p.3.
11 Taxile Delord, 'Le chicard', in *Les Français peints par eux-mêmes*, T.2 (Curmer, 1840), p.570.
12 Delphine de Girardin, *Lettres parisiennes*, in *Œuvres complètes de Mme Emile de Girardin*, T.4 (Plon, 1860), p.378. (Letter of 10.8.1839).
13 Delord, 'Le chicard', p.571.
14 Edmond Texier, *Le Tableau de Paris* (Paulin and Le Chevalier, 1852).
15 Honoré de Balzac, 'Théorie de la démarche' (1833), in *Œuvres diverses*, T.2 (1830–1835), ed. Marcel Bouteron and Henri Longnon (Conard, 1938), p.627.
16 Honoré de Balzac, 'Traité de la vie élégante' (1830), in *Œuvres diverses*, T.2, p.180.
17 Walter Benjamin, *Charles Baudelaire : A Lyric Poet in the Era of High Capitalism*, translated by Harry Zohn (New Left Books, 1973), pp.35–39.
18 Quoted by Benjamin, *Charles Baudelaire*, p.38. See also Louis Wirth, 'Urbanism as a way of life', first published in *American Journal of Sociology*, Vol.44, July 1938, reproduced in *Cities and Society*, edited by Paul K. Hatt and Albert J. Reiss (Glencoe, 1961), pp.46–63, especially pp.54–55.

19 Jules Janin, *Un Hiver à Paris* (Aubert, 1843), p.195. For a further discussion of the important 'partout et nulle part' motif in nineteenth-century writing in Paris, see Richard D.E. Burton, 'The Unseen Seer, or Proteus in the City: Aspects of a Nineteenth-Century Parisian Myth', *French Studies*, 62, 1, January 1988, pp.50–68.
20 Honoré de Balzac, *Facino Cane*, in *La Comédie humaine*, T.4, edited by Pierre Citron (Editions du Seuil, 1966), pp.257–258. The introduction to the story quoted here is clearly autobiographical in character.
21 Charles Baudelaire, 'Le peintre de la vie moderne', in *Œuvres complètes*, T.2, edited by Claude Pichois (Gallimard, 1976), p.692.
22 See Richard D. Burton, *The Context of Baudelaire's 'Le Cygne'*, Durham Modern Language Series, FM 1 (Durham, 1980), p.41.
23 Honoré de Balzac, *Le Cousin Pons*, in *La Comédie humaine*, T.5, p.261.
24 de Girardin, *Lettres parisiennes*, p.393. (Letter of 13.9.1839)

Chapter 2 : Human Hieroglyphs: the role of dress in Parisian life

1 Quoted in Henriette Vanier, *La Mode et ses métiers : frivolités et luttes des classes 1830–1870* (Armand Colin, 1960), p.100.
2 *Le Constitutionnel*, 30.1.1838. quoted in Vanier, *La Mode et ses métiers*, p.96.
3 Quoted in Vanier, *La Mode et ses métiers*, pp.49–50.
4 Quoted in Vanier, *La Mode et ses métiers*, p.168.
5 V.J.E. de Jouy, *L'Hermite de la Chaussée-d'Antin, ou Observations sur les mœurs et usages parisiens au commencement du XIXe siècle* (Pillet, 1815).
6 Quoted in Vanier, *La Mode et ses métiers*, p.14.
7 Lenormant, 'Du costume parisien', p.7.
8 Lenormant, 'Du costume parisien', p.8.
9 L. Montigny, *Le Provincial à Paris, Esquisses des mœurs parisiennes*, T.1 (Ladvocat, 1825), pp.65 and 248.
10 See Burton, *Context*, pp.45–47.
11 Balzac, 'Traite de la vie élégante', p.160.
12 Balzac, 'Traite de la vie élégante', p.161.
13 Baudelaire, *Oeuvres complètes*, T.2, p.711.
14 Roger Kempf, *Dandies : Baudelaire et cie* (Editions du Seuil, 1977), p.9. For first-rate discussions of dandyism, see Emilien Carassus, *Le Mythe du dandy* (Armand Colin, 1971) and Françoise Coblence, *Le Dandysme, obligation d'incertitude* (Presses universitaires de France, 1988)
15 Baudelaire, *Œuvres complètes*, T.2, p.710.
16 Balzac, 'Traité de la vie élégante'.
17 Baudelaire, *Œuvres compètes*, T.2, p.710.

18 Quentin Bell, *On Human Finery* (The Hogarth Press, 1976), especially chapters 6 and 7. See also Philippe Perrot, *Les Dessus et les dessous de la bourgeoisie* (Brussels: Editions Complexe, 1984).
19 Quoted in Vanier, *La Mode et ses métiers*, pp.16–17.
20 Lenormant, 'Du costume parisien', p.15.
21 Baudelaire, 'Salon de 1846', *Œuvres complètes*, T.2, p.494.
22 On changes in Parisian middle-class interiors, see de Girardin, *Lettres parisiennes*, pp.295–296. (Letter of 25.1.1839)
23 de Girardin, *Lettres parisiennes*, pp.271–272. (Letter of 14.12.1838)
24 Quoted in Vanier, *La Mode et ses métiers*, pp.26–27. (Letter of 27.4.1838)
25 de Girardin, *Lettres parisiennes*, pp.448–449. (Letter of 24.1.1840)
26 Honoré de Balzac, *La Cousine Bette*, in *La Comédie humaine*, T.5, p.49.
27 Quoted in Vanier, *La Mode et ses métiers*, p.199.

Chapter 3 : The rise of the *café*

1 François Fosca, *Histoire des cafés de Paris* (Firmin-Didot, 1934), p.14. For further valuable information on cafés, see Henry-Melchior de Lange, *Le Petit Monde des cafés et débits parisiens au XIXe siècle* (Presses universitaires de France, 1990) and Monique Membrado, *Poétique des cafés* (Publisud, 1989).
2 Fournel, *Ce qu'on voit dans les rues de Paris*, p.364.
3 Antoine Caillot, *Mémoires pour servir à l'histoire des mœurs et usages des Français*, T.1 (Dauvin, 1827), p.362.
4 E. and J. de Goncourt, *Histoire de la société française pendant la Révolution* (Flammarion-Fasquelle, no date), pp.188–189.
5 Joseph Mainzer, 'Le cafetier', in *Les Français peints par eux-mêmes*, T.4, (Curmer ,1840), p.295 .
6 Mainzer, 'Le cafetier', p.295.
7 Montigny, *Le Provincial à Paris*, T.2, p.74.
8 *Paris-Fumeur* (Taride, 1855), p.38.
9 See Maurice Agulhon, *Le Cercle dans la France bourgeoise 1810–1848*, *Cahiers des Annales* (Armand Colin, 1977), pp.51–53.
10 Jean-Paul Aron, *Essai sur la sensibilité alimentaire à Paris au 19e siècle*, *Cahiers des Annales* (Armand Colin, 1967), p.17.
11 Jeanne Gaillard, *Paris, la ville 1852–1870* (Honoré Champion, 1977), p.526. The whole distinction between 'introversion' and 'extroversion' is greatly indebted to this work.
12 Caillot, *Mémoires*, T.1, pp.364–365.
13 Mainzer, 'Le cafetier', p.293.
14 Auguste Ricard, 'Le garçon de café', in *Les Français peints par eux-mêmes*, T.2 (Curmer, 1840), p.305.

15 Agulhon, *Le Cercle*, p.55.
16 Agulhon, *Le Cercle*, pp.57 and 71.
17 Agulhon, *Le Cercle*, p.70.
18 For *cabinets de lecture*, see Françoise Parent, 'Le rôle du cabinet de lecture', in *Manuel d'histoire littéraire de la France*, T.4 (1789–1848), 1ere partie (Editions Sociales, 1972), pp.440–445. The role of the Garde Nationale in bourgeois sociability is well brought out in M.A. Bazin (Anaïs de Raucon), *L'Epoque sans nom, Esquisses de Paris 1830–1833*, T.1 (Alexandre Mesnier, 1833), p.50. For freemasonry in Paris at this time, see Pluchonneau aîné, *Physiologie du Franc-Maçon* (Charles Warée, no date).
19 Jules Michelet, *Journal*, T.1 (1828–1848), edited by Paul Viallaneix (Gallimard, 1959), p.291. (Entry dated February 1839)

Chapter 4 : The restaurant

1 Agulhon, *Le Cercle*, p.51.
2 Jean-Paul Aron, *Le Mangeur du 19e siècle* (Denoël, 1976), p.11.
3 Montigny, *Le Provincial à Paris*, T.2, p.119.
4 Quoted in Aron, *Essai sur la sensibilité alimentaire*, pp.16–17.
5 Caillot, *Mémoires*, T.1, pp.356–357.
6 Auguste Luchet, *Paris, esquisses dédiées au peuple parisien* (J. Barbezat, 1830), pp.296–297.
7 Balzac, *Le Cousin Pons, La Comédie humaine*, T.5, p.225.
8 Aron, *Essai sur la sensibilité alimentaire*, p.13.
9 Preface to *Almanach des gourmands* (1804), in Grimod de la Reynière, *Ecrits gastronomiques*, edited by Jean-Claude Sonnet (Union Générale d'Editions, 1978), p.106.
10 Grimod de la Reynière, *Ecrits gastronomiques*, pp.309–311.
11 Honoré de Balzac, 'Monographie du rentier' (1840), in *Œuvres diverses*, T.3, edited by Marcel Bouteron and Henri Longnon (Conard, 1940), p.215.
12 Quoted in Aron, *Le Mangeur*, p.77.
13 Aron, *Le Mangeur*, p.157.

Chapter 5 : *Guinguettes, goguettes* and *marchands de vin*

1 Quoted in Alain Faure, *Paris carême-prenant: Du carnaval à Paris au 19e siècle 1800–1914* (Hachette, 1978), p.17. The whole of this section owes much to this excellent study. For further discussion of the theme of drinking, see Didier Nourrisson, *Le Buveur du XIXe siècle* (Albin Michel, 1990).
2 Caillot, *Mémoires*, pp.373–374.
3 Montigny, *Le Provincial à Paris*, T.1, p.203.

4 Quoted in Faure, *Paris carême-prenant*, p.16.
5 de Jouy, *L'Hermite*, T.1, p.16.
6 Quoted in Faure, *Paris carême-prenant*, p.24.
7 Martin Nadaud, *Mémoires de Léonard, ancien garçon maçon*, edited by Maurice Agulhon (Hachette, 1976), pp.142–143.
8 Alphonse Esquiros, *Les Vierges folles* (E. Dentu, 1873), pp.153–156.
9 Faure, *Paris carême-prenant*, p.16.
10 For an excellent account and analysis of these developments, see Philippe Ariès, *L'Homme devant la mort* (Editions du Seuil, 1977), pp.488–543.
11 For the significance of this development, see Louis Chevalier, *Labouring Classes and Dangerous Classes in Paris in the First Half of the Nineteenth Century*, translated by Frank Jellinek (Routledge and Kegan Paul, 1973), pp.83–88.
12 Victor Hugo, *Les Misérables*, T.2 (Nelson, no date, pp.262–263. (3e partie, I,5)
13 See his *Histoire de la folie à l'âge classique* and also *Surveiller et punir*, to both of which the present argument is indebted.
14 See Roger Caillois, *L'Homme et le sacré* (Gallimard, Idées, 1970), pp.62–63 and Joseph Rykwert, *The Idea of a Town, The Anthropology of Urban Form in Rome, Italy and the Ancient World* (Faber and Faber,1976), *passim*.
15 For a detailed discussion of the old Carrousel, see Burton, *Context*, pp.32–35.
16 Faure, *Paris carême-prenant*, p.17.
17 Montigny, *Le Provincial à Paris*, T.2, pp.95–96.
18 Nadaud, *Mémoires de Léonard*, p.141.
19 Auguste Cochin, *Paris, sa population, son industrie* (1864).
20 Cochin, *Paris*.
21 See Maurice Agulhon, 'Le problème de la culture populaire en France autour de 1848', in *Romantisme*, 9, 1975, p.51.
22 See Wirth, 'Urbanism as a way of life', *passim*.
23 Pierre Pierrard, *La Vie ouvrière à Lille sous le Second Empire* (Bloud et Gay, 1965), p.445. For *goguettes* and the social and political significance of drinking in general in early nineteenth century France, see Richard D.E. Burton, *Baudelaire and the Second Republic. Writing and Revolution* (Oxford: Oxford University Press, 1991), pp.185–219.
24 For the political role of *marchands de vin*, see the fascinating article by Maurice Talmeyr, 'Mœurs électorales: le marchand de vin', *Revue des Deux Mondes*, 15 August 1898, pp.876–891.

25 See John M. Merriman, *The Agony of the Republic, The Repression of the Left in Revolutionary France 1848–1851* (New Haven: Yale University Press, 1978), pp.97–98.
26 L.A. Berthaud, 'Le goguettier', in *Les Français peints par eux-mêmes*, T.4 (Curmer, 1840), p.315.
27 Montigny, *Le Provincial à Paris*, T.3, pp.321–322.
28 Berthaud, 'Le goguettier', p.315.
29 Berthaud, 'Le goguettier', p.317.
30 Montigny, *Le Provincial à Paris*, T.3, pp.322–323.
31 Berthaud, 'Le goguettier', p.315.

Chapter 6 : Shops and Shopping

1 For general information on shops, shopkeepers and shopping, see, *inter alia*, Alain Faure, 'L'épicerie parisienne au XIXe siècle, ou la corporation éclatée', *Mouvement social*, N°108, juillet-septembre 1979, pp.113–130. For *grands magasins*, see Gaillard, *Paris, la ville*, pp.525–558 and Michael B. Miller, *The 'Bon Marché' : Bourgeois Culture and the Department Store 1869–1920* (Princeton: Princeton University Press, 1981).
2 Grimod de la Reynière, *Ecrits gastronomiques*, p.237.
3 Montigny, *Le Provincial à Paris*, T.3, pp.233–235.
4 Honoré de Balzac, 'Ce qui disparaît de Paris' (1844), in *Œuvres diverses*, T.3 (1836–1848), edited by Marcel Bouteron and Henri Longnon (Conard, 1940), p.608.
5 Charles Vincent, 'Les dernières échoppes', in *Paris-Guide par les principaux écrivains et artistes de la France*, T.2 (Brussels: A. Lacroix, Verbroeckhoven et Cie, 1867), p.972.
6 For a useful study of the structural evolution of the nineteenth century Parisian shop, see Claudine Reinharez and Josselyne Chamarat, *Boutiques du temps passé* (Presses de la Connaissance 1977).
7 Grimod de la Reynière, *Ecrits gastronomiques*, p.235.
8 Montigny, *Le Provincial à Paris*, T.2, p.152.
9 Caillot, *Mémoires*, T.2, pp.218–219.
10 Honoré de Balzac, *César Birotteau, La Comédie humaine*, T.4, p.140.
11 Honoré de Balzac, *Gaudissart II, La Comédie humaine*, T.5, p.356.
12 Sébastien Mercier, *Tableau de Paris*, T.5 (Amsterdam, 1782), p.13.
13 Quoted in Louis Hautecœur, *Histoire de l'architecture classique en France*, T.6: *La Restauration et le gouvernement de juillet 1815–1848* (Picard, 1955), p.139.
14 Touchard Lafosse, *Histoire de Paris*, T.2 (Dion et Lambert, 1853), p.929.

NOTES AND REFERENCES 77

15 Maxime du Camp, *Paris, ses organes, ses fonctions et sa vie*, T.6 (Hachette, 1875), pp.322–323.
16 For the economic organisation of the *grands magasins*, see Gaillard, *Paris, la ville*, pp.525–558.
17 For a useful history of shops under the Restoration and Bourgeois Monarchy, see Hautecœur, *Histoire de l'architecture classique*, T.6, pp.139–141.
18 Balzac, *Gaudissart II*, p.356.
19 Balzac, *Gaudissart II*, p.357.
20 Amédée Kermel, 'Les passages de Paris', in *Le Livre des cent-et-un*, T.10 (Frankfurt: Schmerber, 1833), pp.37–47.
21 Gaillard, *Paris, la ville*, p.526.
22 Texier, *Le Tableau de Paris*, T.2, p.277.
23 Caillot, *Mémoires*, T.2, pp.219–220.
24 Lafosse, *Histoire de Paris*, T.2, p.927.
25 Eugène Suë, *Les Mystères de Paris* (Pauvert, 1963), p.329.
26 Arnould Frémy, 'La revendeuse à la toilette', in *Les Français peints par eux-mêmes* (1840). Quoted in Vanier, *La Mode et ses métiers*, p.132.

Chapter 7 : The Omnibus

1   de Girardin, *Lettres parisiennes*, p.341. (Letter of May 1839)
2   Poumiès de la Siboutie, *Souvenirs d'un médecin de Paris* (Plon, 1910), p.194.
3   Agulhon, *Le Cercle*, p.51.
4   Texier, *Le Tableau de Paris*.
5   *Paris-en-omnibus* (Alphonse Taride , 1854), p.11 .
6   Fournel, *Esquisses et croquis parisiens*, 2e serie (Plon, 1879), p.24.
7   *Paris-en-omnibus*, pp.54–55.
8   Texier, *Le Tableau de Paris*,.
9   Horace Raïsson, *Histoire de la police de Paris* (B. Dusillon, 1844), p.307.
10 J. and E. de Goncourt, *Manette Salomon* (Flammarion-Fasquelle, no date), p.191.
11 *Paris-en-omnibus*, pp.78–79.

Chapter 8 : *Bals publics*

1   Faure, *Paris carême-prenant*, p.45.
2   Texier, *Le Tableau de Paris*, T.2, p.175.
3   Quoted in Faure, *Paris carême-prenant*, p.90.
4   Delord, 'Le chicard', p.364.
5   *Vieux souvenirs de Mgr. le Prince de Joinville 1818–1848* (Mercure de France, 1970), p.159.

6 Victor Rozier, *Les Bals publics à Paris* (Gustave Havard, 1855), p. 50.
7 Louis Véron, *Mémoires d'un bourgeois de Paris*, T.3 (Librairie Nouvelle, 1857), p.388.
8 Delord, 'Le chicard', p.371.
9 Jules Janin, *Un hiver à Paris* (1846). Quoted in Faure, *Paris carême-prenant*, p.53.
10 de Girardin, *Lettres parisiennes*, p.51. (Letter of 11.1.1837)
11 Quoted in Faure, *Paris carême-prenant*, p.53.
12 Veron, *Mémoires*, T.3, p.388. For the growth of a 'counterculture of the young' after 1830, see Anthony Esler, 'Youth in revolt : the French generation of 1830', in *Modern European Social History*, edited by Robert J. Bezucha (D.C. Heath and Co., Lexington, Mass., 1972), pp.301–334.
13 Delord, 'Le chicard', p.370.
14 Heinrich Heine, *Lutèce* (Michel Levy, 1863), p.241.
15 de Girardin, *Lettres parisiennes*, p.249. (Letter of 15.3.1838)
16 Honoré de Balzac, *Un prince de la Bohème*, *La Comédie humaine*, T.5, p.279.
17 *Paris-dansant* (Dupont, 1845), p.7–10.
18 Heine, *Lutèce*, p.233.

Chapter 9 : Carnival

1 Faure, *Paris carême-prenant*, p.89.
2 Michael R. Marrus, 'Social drinking in the belle époque', *Journal of Social History*, Vol.7, N° 2, Winter 1974, pp.115–141.
3 Faure, *Paris carême-prenant*, p.120.
4 Quoted in Faure, *Paris carême-prenant*, p.126.
5 Hugo, *Les Misérables*, T.4, p.332. (5ᵉ partie, VI, 1)
6 Texier, *Le Tableau de Paris*, T.1, p.54.
7 *Journal de Delécluze 1824–1828*, edited by Robert Baschet (Bernard Grasset, 1948), pp.124–125.
8 Hugo, *Les Misérables*, T.4, p.332. (5ᵉ partie, VI, 1)
9 Faure, *Paris carême-prenant*, p.47.
10 de Girardin, *Lettres parisiennes*, p.57. (Letter of 8.2.1837)

Chapter 10 : *Saltimbanques* and prostitutes

1 Théodore Faucher, *Histoire du Boulevard du Temple, depuis son origine jusqu'à sa démolition* (E. Dentu, 1863), p.48.
2 Faucher, *Histoire*, p.60.
3 Gérard de Nerval, 'Le Boulevard du Temple, autrefois et aujourd'hui' (1844), in *Variétés et fantaisies*, edited by Jean Richer (M.J. Minard, 1964), p.69.

4 Gérard de Nerval, 'La comédie des singes' (1846), in *Variétés et fantaisies*, p.89.
5 Texier, *Le Tableau de Paris*, T.1, pp.246–247.
6 Gustave Flaubert, *Par les champs et par les grèves* (Lausanne: Editions Rencontre, 1964), pp.332–333.
7 Fournel, *Esquisses et croquis parisiens*, 1ere série, p.288.
8 For a searching discussion of the significance of these works, see T.J. Clark, *The Absolute Bourgeois, Artists and Politics in France 1848–1851* (Thames and Hudson, 1973), pp.120–123.
9 Emile Zola, 'Lettres parisiennes', *La Cloche* 8.6.1872, in *Œuvres complétes*, edited by Henri Mitterand, T.14 (Cercle du Livre Précieux, 1970), p.79.
10 Fournel, *Esquisses et croquis parisiens*, 1ere série, p.173.
11 For official policy towards prostitution under the Bourgeois Monarchy, see Alain Corbin, *Les Filles de noce, misère sexuelle et prostitution (19e et 20e siècles)* (Aubier Montaigne, 1978), especially pp.17–26.
12 Esquiros, *Les Vierges folles*, pp.2–3.
13 Texier, *Le Tableau de Paris*, T.2, p.57.
14 *Journal des Goncourt*, T.2 edited by Robert Ricatte (Fasquelle-Flammarion, 1956) p.11.
15 Alain Corbin, 'La Prostituée', in *Misérable et glorieuse. La femme du 19e siècle*, edited by Jean-Paul Aron (Fayard, 1980), p.54.
16 *Le Nain jaune* 10.3.1866. Quoted in Henri Gaillard, *Emile Augier et la comédie sociale* (Bernard Grasset, 1910), p.47.
17 *Journal des Goncourt*, T.1, p.1019.
18 For a further discussion of these ideas, see Burton, *Context*, pp.42–50.

Chapter 11: Conclusion: 'Public' and 'Private' in pre–1850 Paris

1 Balzac, 'Ce qui disparaît de Paris', p.607.
2 Quoted in Adeline Daumard, 'Progrès et prise de conscience des classes moyennes', in *Histoire économique et sociale de la France*, T.3, 2e volume, edited by Fernand Braudel et Ernest Labrousse (Presses universitaires de France, 1976), p.897.
3 Quoted in Guy P. Paimade, *Capitalisme et capitalistes français au 19e siècle* (Armand Colin, 1961), p.63.
4 Honoré de Balzac, *Melmoth réconcilié*, La Comédie humaine, T.6, P 530.
5 Honoré de Balzac, *Ferragus*, La Comédie humaine, T.4, p.00.
6 For a summary of this major development, see Burton, *Context*, pp.36–38.
7 Gaillard, *Paris, la ville*, p.525.
8 M.A. Bazin, *L'Epoque sans nom*, T.2, pp.141–45 *passim*.

9   Honoré de Balzac, *La Fille aux yeux d'or, La Comédie humaine*, T.4, p.104.
10 On the need for bourgeois males to carry a cane, see Bazin, *L'Époque sans nom*, T.1, p.39.
11 de Girardin, *Lettres parisiennes*, pp.140–143. (Letter of 12.7.1837)
12 Balzac, 'Ce qui disparaît de Paris', p.608.
13 *Journal des Goncourt*, T.2, p.226.
14 Victor Hugo, *Choses vues, Souvenirs, journaux, cahiers 1847–1848*, edited by Hubert Juin (Gallimard Folio, 1972), pp.104–106.
15 Peter H. Amann, *Revolution and Mass Democracy, The Paris Club Movement in 1848* (Princeton: Princeton University Press, 1975), p.xiii.
16 Charles de Rémusat, *Mémoires de ma vie*, T.4 (1841–1851), edited by Charles-Henri Pouthas (Plon, 1962), p.312.
17 de Rémusat, *Mémoires*, T.4, p.345.
18 Marcel Cornu, *La Conquête de Paris* (Mercure de France, 1972), p.38.
19 Emile Zola, *La Curée, Œuvres complètes*, T.2, pp.158–459.
20 See Burton, *Context*, pp.12–17.
21 Delvau, *Les Dessous de Paris*, p.134.
22 Michelle Perrot, 'La femme populaire rebelle', in *L'Histoire sans qualités*, edited by Christiane Dufrancatel *et aliae* (Editions Galilée, 1979), p.144.
23 Richard Sennett, *The Fall of Public Man* (Cambrdige: Cambridge University Press, 1976), chapters 7, 8, 9.

EU authorised representative for GPSR:
Easy Access System Europe, Mustamäe tee 50,
10621 Tallinn, Estonia
gpsr.requests@easproject.com